BRIAN GREUTMAN

Delighting in the Lord Through the Psalms II
Copyright 2018 Brian M. Greutman
All rights reserved

Greutman, Brian, 1973-, author
Delighting in the Lord: through the Psalms II/Brian Greutman
ISBN 978-1-64316-765-7

Design by Todd Schlosser / www.ledstudios.com
Printed by Diggy POD, Tecumseh, Michigan

All Scripture quotations, unless otherwise indicated, are taken
from the Holy Bible, New International Version®, NIV®. Copyright
©1973, 1978, 1984, 2011 by Biblica, Inc.™ Used by permission of
Zondervan. All rights reserved worldwide. www.zondervan.com
The "NIV" and "New International Version" are trademarks
registered in the United States Patent and Trademark Office by
Biblica, Inc.™

Scripture quotations marked "ESV" are from the ESV® Bible (The
Holy Bible, English Standard Version®), copyright © 2001 by
Crossway, a publishing ministry of Good News Publishers. Used by
permission. All rights reserved.

Table of Contents

Acknowledgements

This entire project wouldn't be possible without the help of many people. Thanks to my wonderful wife Gretchen for putting up with all the late nights, crazy schedule, and endless questions as I worked on this project. Thanks for your support and patience. I love you! Nathan, Nicholas, and Noah, thanks for being incredible sons. It is a joy to watch you play baseball and all of your other activities. Most of all, it is a pleasure to watch you grow in your faith.

Thanks to Todd Schlosser for doing the artwork, layout, and design for this book. Your talents are amazing! I so appreciate your creativity, expertise, and support for the vision of this project.

I'm so grateful for the following people who helped edit this book: Pastor Dennis Sawyer, Pastor Brett Hollis, and John Van Lierop Jr. I appreciate the time and effort you spent once again to enable the message of "Delighting in the Lord" to be a blessing to many!

Thanks to my parents Marrell and Terry Greutman for your constant support and love. I'm thankful for your example of "Delighting in the Lord"! Thanks to my sister Heidi-Lyn and brother-in-law Dan Mensonides for your encouragement.

Thanks to Pastor Andy Rosas and Riverview Community Church for your support and love. It has been a pleasure leading the people of Riverview in worship for the last fifteen years and I look forward to the future!

It has been a pleasure working with the Riverview Community Church staff over the years. Thanks to Pastor Andy Rosas, Ron Lalime, and Lyndsay Martin for your friendship and partnership in ministry. The Riverview Worship Team has been a blessing to lead and serve alongside for fifteen years. Your dedication to the Lord and worshiping him inspires me!

Thanks to my prayer partners Russell Booth and Jeff Fiorito fifteen years and counting!

Thanks to Arrow Leadership for continuing to support, encourage, and challenge me as a leader in ministry. Thanks to Dr. Steve Brown, Gretchen Englund, and Dr. Sharon Simmonds in particular-thanks for believing in this project!

Preface

Leading up to this project I wondered if there might be a follow-up project to *Delighting in the Lord Through the Psalms*. During my personal devotions, I found myself being encouraged and challenged by the message of Psalms that weren't included in the first project. I felt the Lord leading me to proceed.

As I began to work on this devotional in February of 2017 and the coming months, I found that I was exhausted from the busy schedule we had been keeping with our many activities. In the midst of all the busyness, I ironically felt bored at the same time. As I began to write these devotionals, seeking to delight in the Lord through his Word, I found myself refreshed, encouraged, and inspired once again.

These daily devotionals are divided into six weeks and three bonus days for a total of forty-five entries. Each day includes a Psalm reading, devotional, two reflection questions, and a prayer. The accompanying piano CD has forty-five corresponding compositions with titles that match the devotionals. The track number is given at the start of each devotional. You can listen to each song in the background as you read the corresponding devotional or listen to the CD on its own. (Which I hope you do!)

My prayer is that your love for the Lord would grow as you read these Psalms and devotionals, seeking to delight in the Lord through his Word. May he fill you with his joy, strength, and encouragement as you seek to delight in him!

WEEK

1

DAY 1  Disc 1 / Track 1

The Lord Reigns on High

Why do the nations conspire and the peoples plot in vain? The kings of the earth rise up and the rulers band together against the LORD and against his anointed, saying, "Let us break their chains and throw off their shackles." The One enthroned in heaven laughs; the Lord scoffs at them. He rebukes them in his anger and terrifies them in his wrath, saying, "I have installed my king on Zion, my holy mountain." I will proclaim the LORD's decree: He said to me, "You are my son; today I have become your father. Ask me, and I will make the nations your inheritance, the ends of the earth your possession. You will break them with a rod of iron; you will dash them to pieces like pottery." Therefore, you kings, be wise; be warned, you rulers of the earth. Serve the LORD with fear and celebrate his rule with trembling. Kiss his son, or he will be angry and your way will lead to your destruction, for his wrath can flare up in a moment. Blessed are all who take refuge in him.

PSALM 2:1-12

In this Psalm, earthly kings and rulers rise up against the Lord and his anointed. Why would they do such a thing? Looking back over history this seems to be a pattern. There is something in each of us that resists following God and submitting to his authority. It is evidenced in the way children disobey their parents from an early age. No one teaches us to say, "no". It is part of our sin nature passed onto us from Adam and Eve.

The Lord's response to these rulers in this Psalm is laughter (vs. 4). He rebukes them in anger saying, "I have installed my king on Zion, my holy mountain" (v. 6). This king referred to is a prophecy concerning Jesus who is to come. The Father will give the nations to Jesus as his inheritance as he will come to save us from our sins.

The earthly rulers and kings are told to respect the Lord and his son if they want good success and protection (vs. 12). How can we develop this respect for the Lord? I have noticed that when children get an understanding of the greatness and glory of the Lord it changes the way they respond to him. They honor and respect him for who he is. Then they naturally call out to him for help in troubled times. The same is true for all of us.

Those who take refuge in the Lord will be blessed (vs. 12) and the byproduct is joy. "But let all who take refuge in you be glad; let them ever sing for joy. Spread your protection over them, that those who love your name may rejoice in you" (Ps. 5:11). We, like these earthly rulers, would be wise to seek the Lord for protection; but, more importantly, to esteem and honor him for his greatness and glory.

Reflection Questions

1. Have you ever resisted following the Lord? What was the outcome?

2. In what areas of your life do you currently need to seek the Lord for help?

Lord, forgive me for heart attitudes of "rising up" against you. In light of your greatness and glory, I know you are worthy of my honor, respect, and love. I seek your protection and help today, asking you to fill me with your joy.

DAY 2   Disc 1 / Track 2

The Light of Your Face

Answer me when I call to you, my righteous God. Give me relief from my distress; have mercy on me and hear my prayer. How long will you people turn my glory into shame? How long will you love delusions and seek false gods? Know that the LORD has set apart his faithful servant for himself; the LORD hears when I call to him. Tremble and do not sin; when you are on your beds, search your hearts and be silent. Offer the sacrifices of the righteous and trust in the LORD. Many, LORD, are asking, "Who will bring us prosperity?" Let the light of your face shine on us. Fill my heart with joy when their grain and new wine abound. In peace I will lie down and sleep, for you alone, LORD, make me dwell in safety.

PSALM 4:1-8

Do you ever woner if God hears your cries for help? In this Psalm, David is asking the Lord to answer him, give him relief, have mercy on him, and to hear his prayer (vs. 1). There are times when I feel overwhelmed with stress, anxiety, and trouble and, like David, find myself asking the Lord for the same things.

David expresses frustration with the people around him and their lack of response to God. They may have been slandering him or simply looking to him instead of the Lord when troubles came their way.[1] I also have trouble understanding why people don't acknowledge the Lord in their lives, and I certainly can get upset if they are saying bad things about me. In times like that, I sometimes treat them with impatience, frustration, and lack of love.

However, verse four says, "Know that the Lord has set apart his faithful servant for himself; the Lord hears when I call to him." What an amazing promise-those who seek the Lord are set apart by God for himself and that he hears their prayers! The Lord of heaven cares about our needs and sets us apart to know and love him. We don't have to worry about things-we can trust him!

The psalmist goes on to say, "Many, Lord, are asking, 'Who will bring us prosperity?' Let the light of your face shine on us" (vs. 6). It seems that some people were getting frustrated with King David and their perceived lack of prosperity.[2] King David chooses to pray this little prayer: "Let the light of your face shine on us" (vs. 6). When the light of God's face shines on us it changes everything. This figurative expression signifies the spiritual reality of God's favor being on us. What a great prayer for us to pray!

Moses asked to see the Lord and he was told that he couldn't see God's face and live. He was allowed to look at the Lord's back from a cleft of a rock. After that time, he was glowing as he went around the community.[3] People knew he had been with the Lord. When God's face shines on us (figuratively) people know that we've been with the Lord.

In the final verses of this Psalm, David expresses that his confidence and joy are in the Lord. He asks the Lord to fill him with joy when those around him prosper. It's easy to get jealous of others when they succeed but the psalmist reminds us of what is most important. Where or to whom do we look to for our first joy in life?

Jonathan Edwards said, "The enjoyment of God is the only happiness with which our souls can be satisfied. To go to heaven, fully to enjoy God, is infinitely better than the most pleasant accommodations here. Fathers and mothers, husbands, wives, or children, or the company of earthly friends, are but shadows; but God is the substance. These are but scattered beams, but God is the sun."[4]

Do we believe these words? More importantly, has the truth they convey gotten into our hearts? Once we realize that only God can satisfy-our priorities change. We esteem him above all else. We truly delight in the Lord.

Reflection Questions

1. What is your response to the following verse? "Know that the Lord has set apart his faithful servant for himself; the Lord hears when I call to him" (vs. 4).

2. Do you believe that only the Lord can truly satisfy you? If so, think of a practical example from your life.

Lord, let the light of your face shine on me today. I ask for your help and favor in my life. When people wrong me or attack me, help me trust in you. I know that only you can satisfy my soul. Teach me how to delight in you today.

DAY 3   Disc 1 / Track 3

My Soul is in Anguish

LORD, do not rebuke me in your anger or discipline me in your wrath. Have mercy on me, LORD, for I am faint; heal me, LORD, for my bones are in agony. My soul is in deep anguish. How long, LORD, how long? Turn, LORD, and deliver me; save me because of your unfailing love. Among the dead no one proclaims your name. Who praises you from the grave? I am worn out from my groaning. All night long I flood my bed with weeping and drench my couch with tears. My eyes grow weak with sorrow; they fail because of all my foes. Away from me, all you who do evil, for the LORD has heard my weeping. The Lord has heard my cry for mercy; the Lord accepts my prayer. All my enemies will be overwhelmed with shame and anguish; they will turn back and suddenly be put to shame.

PSALM 6:1-10

Have you ever been overwhelmed with sadness about something? In this Psalm, David is asking God for help and mercy. He seems to be asking for healing from a physical ailment or disease and he doesn't want to die.[5]

David is asking the Lord to deliver him, and he says, "Among the dead no one proclaims your name. Who praises you from the grave?" (v. 5). He is asking the Lord to keep him alive, so he can worship him. Then he mentions his groaning, his tears, and his enemies. He is in great anguish.

There have been times in my life when I was overcome with sadness over my sin or over the struggles of others. I have cried out to the Lord. There have also been times when I've been filled with compassion for those around me when they are going through a difficult situation. In those times, I am reminded of my own need for grace and mercy from the Lord. It can be easy to draw conclusions about another person's situation when things are going well for us. However, it's amazing how our outlook changes when we experience tough times.

This reminds me of the story of Job and how his friends came to offer him consolation after the loss of his children, servants, animals, and health. They made assumptions about why Job was experiencing these trials. They thought it was because of some sin he had committed. In moments like these, it is probably best to simply listen and be supportive of people. Less is more.

In this Psalm, the Lord hears David's cries for mercy, and he hears our cries as well. Hebrews 4:16 says, "Let us then approach God's throne of grace with confidence, so that we may receive mercy and find grace to help us in our time of need." We can boldly come to the Lord asking for his grace and mercy-especially in our time of need.

Reflection Questions

1. Have you ever been overcome with sadness? Where did you turn for support?
2. Who might the Lord be prompting you to help and support in their time of need?

Lord, I cry out to you for mercy and grace in my time of need. I come with confidence knowing that you've promised to help me. I also want to be a support and blessing to others in their time of need. Open my eyes to those opportunities around me.

DAY 4 — Disc 1 / Track 4

Joy for the Needy

I will give thanks to you, LORD, with all my heart; I will tell of all your wonderful deeds. I will be glad and rejoice in you; I will sing the praises of your name, O Most High. My enemies turn back; they stumble and perish before you. For you have upheld my right and my cause, sitting enthroned as the righteous judge. You have rebuked the nations and destroyed the wicked; you have blotted out their name for ever and ever. Endless ruin has overtaken my enemies, you have uprooted their cities; even the memory of them has perished. The LORD reigns forever; he has established his throne for judgment. He rules the world in righteousness and judges the peoples with equity. The LORD is a refuge for the oppressed, a stronghold in times of trouble. Those who know your name trust in you, for you, LORD, have never forsaken those who seek you. Sing the praises of the Lord, enthroned in Zion; proclaim among the nations what he has done. For he who avenges blood remembers; he does not ignore the cries of the afflicted. LORD, see how my enemies persecute me! Have mercy and lift me up from the gates of death, that I may declare your praises in the gates of Daughter Zion, and there rejoice in your salvation.

PSALM 9:1-14

Do you ever feel bored with life? Are there times when you struggle to find things to be excited or joyful about? After an amazing vacation or big event, I often have a hard time getting back into the daily grind of life. This Psalm tells us ways and reasons to be filled with joy.

The first way is to be thankful and to tell of the Lord's wonderful deeds. It's amazing how gratitude shifts our focus from what we don't have to that for which we can be thankful. The Lord has been good to my family in so many ways. This fills me with joy when I think about it. Then there are the countless ways I see him at work in the lives of those around me. That isn't even considering his amazing works told in the Bible. These are all reasons to joyfully sing praises to the Lord.

Then David speaks of God coming to his defense and judging his enemies when they attack. He also describes the Lord as the righteous and equitable judge. Verse ten says, "Those who know your name trust in you, for you, Lord, have never forsaken those who seek you." When we truly know the Lord, we can trust him. We know that his decisions are for the best and that he won't ever leave those who seek him.

One theme that gets repeated in this Psalm is the Lord's help for the afflicted and the needy. The Lord's heart is turned towards us in our time of need. "The Lord is close to the brokenhearted and saves those who are crushed in spirit" (Ps. 34:18).

I think of times when one of our boys need me to help them with homework, do a task, or pay attention to them. Sometimes I am attentive to them and other times I blow the opportunity because I'm too focused on other things.

Thankfully the Lord is not like me in that he is never too busy to hear the cries and needs of his children. This fills me with hope, encouragement, and joy! We can trust that the Lord of all creation hears our every cry and need.

Reflection Questions

1. What are you most thankful for today? How can this fill you with joy?
2. Do you believe that God is always attentive to the needs of his children? If so, how does it affect you?

Lord, I am filled with gratitude for your many blessings in my life. I am filled with joy as I think about them. Thank you for being my help in time of need and for always taking time for me. I purpose to follow your example in the way I treat others.

DAY 5 Disc 1 / Track 5

Flawless Words

Help, LORD, for no one is faithful anymore; those who are loyal have vanished from the human race. Everyone lies to their neighbor; they flatter with their lips but harbor deception in their hearts. May the LORD silence all flattering lips and every boastful tongue—those who say, "By our tongues we will prevail; our own lips will defend us—who is lord over us?" "Because the poor are plundered and the needy groan, I will now arise," says the LORD. "I will protect them from those who malign them." And the words of the Lord are flawless, like silver purified in a crucible, like gold refined seven times. You, LORD, will keep the needy safe and will protect us forever from the wicked, who freely strut about when what is vile is honored by the human race.

PSALM 12:1-8

In the months prior to the 2016 presidential election in the United States it seemed that basic decency had gone by the wayside. There was so much negativity, polarization, and pettiness, that it was extremely discouraging.

Perhaps that is how David felt when he wrote this Psalm. He says that faithful and loyal people cannot be found. In fact, he says that people are lying to each other left and right. That sounds familiar! The end of verse two says, "they flatter with their lips but harbor deception in their hearts." They would say one thing to people's face while hiding how they really felt.

Before we pass along judgement it's important to ask if we've ever done that. I know that I have, and I am not proud of it. David then calls on the Lord to silence the flattery, deception, and those trusting in their own strength.

"'Because the poor are plundered and the needy groan, I will now arise,' says the Lord. 'I will protect them from those who malign them'" (v. 5). God cares about those in need and will act on their behalf.

Right after this statement the psalmist says that God's words are flawless. This is in stark contrast to all the flattery, lying, and deceptive words David saw, and we see around us today. God's words are not only true, but he always delivers on his promises. We know his words are powerful, as he spoke the world into existence.

At the end of the Psalm it says that the Lord will protect us from the wicked who "freely strut about" (v. 8) when evil is held in high esteem. What an encouraging thought for us today. When evil is lifted high, the Lord promises to protect us from evildoers. We must remember that our confidence and hope are ultimately not in the people around us. (including politicians, friends, family, etc.) Our hope and confidence are in the Lord and his flawless words.

Reflection Questions
1.   Have you ever resorted to flattery in your speech? If so, why and what was the result?
2.   Why is the statement "the words of the Lord are flawless" (v. 6) so significant?

Father, I purpose to use my words to please you, encourage others, and to be truthful. Guard me from flattery and deception in my speech. I am thankful that your words are flawless and that your promises are true.

DAY 6   Disc 1 / Track 6

Unshakeable

LORD, who may dwell in your sacred tent? Who may live on your holy mountain? The one whose walk is blameless, who does what is righteous, who speaks the truth from their heart; whose tongue utters no slander, who does no wrong to a neighbor, and casts no slur on others; who despises a vile person but honors those who fear the LORD; who keeps an oath even when it hurts, and does not change their mind; who lends money to the poor without interest; who does not accept a bribe against the innocent. Whoever does these things will never be shaken.

PSALM 15:1-5

Do you want to be a person who is close to the Lord and stays true to your commitments? If so, this Psalm gives a recipe for doing that.

First, we need to be people of integrity who seek to do the right thing. We need to be people of our word (v. 2). Unfortunately, this is becoming less of the norm in our society, but it is vitally important.

Next, we need to speak the truth and not slander others with our words (v. 3). James 3:9-10 says, "With the tongue we praise our Lord and Father, and with it we curse human beings, who have been made in God's likeness. Out of the same mouth come praise and cursing. My brothers and sisters, this should not be."

Ferguson writes in *The Power of Words and the Wonder of God*, "We were created as [in] the image of God to bless God. It is blatant hypocrisy, double-mindedness, and sin to bless God and then casually curse those who have been made as his very likeness."[6]

When we use our tongues to harm others, it hurts our witness for the Lord. We need to be as consistent as possible with our speech. While writing this, I got frustrated with our boys as they were working on homework, getting ready for bed, and not listening well. In my irritation and impatience, I said some things to them that were less than kind. Ironically, as I was writing a devotional about the importance of using our words to bless others, I didn't do a good job myself. So...God is speaking to me through this devotional.

The psalmist goes on to mention those who despise evil people but honor those who "fear the Lord" (v. 4). We need to have a respect for those who love the Lord. I think of the many people who have been an encouragement and example to me in my life. Many of them have been mentors who have given me advice and wisdom along the way.

He also stresses the importance of keeping our word "even when it hurts" (vs. 4). This can be difficult. When my wife Gretchen and I ask our kids if they want to sign-up for sports, choir, or other extra-curricular activities we tell them that they are committing until the end of the season or activity. Whether they like the activity or not, they must continue until the end. The truth is, we as parents are committing to it as well.

The last qualities mentioned in this Psalm are giving to the poor and not taking a bribe against innocent people (v. 5). If we do all these things, this Psalm says we will be unshakeable. That is the kind of person I want to be!

Reflection Questions

1. Are you a person of your word? If not, how can you improve in that area?
2. How can hurtful speech about others negatively affect our witness for the Lord?

Lord, I want to be close to you and be unshakeable in my commitments. I choose to be a person of my word. Help me to use my words to build people up and not tear them down so I can be a good reflection of you.

DAY 7 ☀ Disc 1 / Track 7

The Path to Eternity

Hear me, LORD, my plea is just; listen to my cry. Hear my prayer—it does not rise from deceitful lips. Let my vindication come from you; may your eyes see what is right. Though you probe my heart, though you examine me at night and test me, you will find that I have planned no evil; my mouth has not transgressed. Though people tried to bribe me, I have kept myself from the ways of the violent through what your lips have commanded. My steps have held to your paths; my feet have not stumbled. I call on you, my God, for you will answer me; turn your ear to me and hear my prayer. Show me the wonders of your great love, you who save by your right hand those who take refuge in you from their foes. Keep me as the apple of your eye; hide me in the shadow of your wings from the wicked who are out to destroy me, from my mortal enemies who surround me. By your hand save me from such people, LORD, from those of this world whose reward is in this life. May what you have stored up for the wicked fill their bellies; may their children gorge themselves on it, and may there be leftovers for their little ones. As for me, I will be vindicated and will see your face; when I awake, I will be satisfied with seeing your likeness.

PSALM 17:1-9, 14-15

This Psalm is a cry to God for help based on David's life of seeking after the Lord. He says, "My steps have held to your paths" (v. 5). This reminds me of the first chapter of Psalms which says that the person who delights in the law of the Lord, will be blessed or happy in life. If we do that, the Lord listens to us when we pray (v. 6). Verse eight says, "Keep me as the apple of your eye; hide me in the shadow of your wings...". What an incredible expression of God's love and protection for us.

I love my wife Gretchen and our boys and would do anything to protect them from danger. When they are in trouble or physical danger is near, I jump at the opportunity to help them. The same is true, but in greater ways, of our Heavenly Father. He listens to our prayers, protects us, and longs to show us his love.

In verse fourteen David is asking God to save him from the wicked "...whose reward is in this life". What a telling statement! Those who don't know the Lord only have this life (e.g. riches, power, and relationships) to live for. They have no higher purpose.

David longs for the day when he will see the Lord face to face being satisfied in him (v. 15). David knew this life is but a blip on the radar, and it doesn't compare with an eternity of looking on the Lord's face and seeing his greatness! We will be completely satisfied in the Lord forever and this life and its struggles are preparation for that. Our struggles on this Earth can increase our love for the Lord and dependency on him.

As we learn to find our joy first in the Lord here and now, we place more value on eternity than we do on the fleeting pleasures of this world.[7]

Reflection Questions

1. Do you believe that God loves you and considers you the apple of his eye (v. 8)? If so, how should that affect you?
2. Do you look forward to being in the presence of the Lord for eternity? If so, how should that change your current priorities?

Father, I look forward to being in your presence for eternity. I choose to make eternal things the top priority in my life now. I know as I do, you will fill me with your joy.

WEEK

2

DAY 1 ⚜ ◉ Disc 1 / Track 8

The Lord Gives Victory

May the LORD answer you when you are in distress; may the name of the God of Jacob protect you. May he send you help from the sanctuary and grant you support from Zion. May he remember all your sacrifices and accept your burnt offerings. May he give you the desire of your heart and make all your plans succeed. May we shout for joy over your victory and lift up our banners in the name of our God. May the LORD grant all your requests. Now this I know: The LORD gives victory to his anointed. He answers him from his heavenly sanctuary with the victorious power of his right hand. Some trust in chariots and some in horses, but we trust in the name of the LORD our God. They are brought to their knees and fall, but we rise up and stand firm. LORD, give victory to the king! Answer us when we call!

PSALM 20:1-9

Do you believe that God longs to bless you and give you success in this life? In this Psalm David is preparing for battle[8] as he asks the Lord to give him victory. Much of this Psalm is written as if the people are speaking to King David, as they ask for the Lord's help. They want the Lord to remember David's faithfulness and to give him his heart's desire in making him successful.

Sometimes we forget that the Lord longs to bless us. If we are seeking first his kingdom (Matt. 6:33) and his glory, our desires will be increasingly conformed to his. We long to please him.

In this Psalm, they are already speaking of shouting to God for victory and lifting up banners in his name (v. 5). Their desire is to give God glory for what he is about to do! They understand that the Lord gives success to those who honor and acknowledge him.

Verse seven says, "Some trust in chariots and some in horses, but we trust in the name of the Lord our God." What an amazing statement. David showed this kind of trust when he faced the giant Goliath. He said, "You come against me with sword and spear and javelin, but I come against you in the name of the Lord Almighty..." (I Sam. 17:45). David knew that victory would only come by trusting in the Lord.

How often do we fight our battles in our own strength? As a pastor, I must constantly ask myself if I am relying on God for direction and help; or am I depending on something else? It's easy to begin to rely on our own abilities in the areas of our giftedness; however, our own gifts only go so far. May the Lord give us victory as we trust in him!

Reflection Questions

1. Has God ever given you victory in a battle? Think about that time.
2. Why are we tempted to rely on our own strength or possessions rather than on God?

Lord, you give victory to your people as they rely on you. I put my trust in you today asking for victory in the battles I am facing. I will acknowledge your greatness and glory as the victorious God!

DAY 2   Disc 1 / Track 9

The Joy of Your Presence

The king rejoices in your strength, LORD. How great is his joy in the victories you give! You have granted him his heart's desire and have not withheld the request of his lips. You came to greet him with rich blessings and placed a crown of pure gold on his head. He asked you for life, and you gave it to him— length of days, for ever and ever. Through the victories you gave, his glory is great; you have bestowed on him splendor and majesty. Surely you have granted him unending blessings and made him glad with the joy of your presence. For the king trusts in the LORD; through the unfailing love of the Most High he will not be shaken. Your hand will lay hold on all your enemies; your right hand will seize your foes. When you appear for battle, you will burn them up as in a blazing furnace. The LORD will swallow them up in his wrath and his fire will consume them. You will destroy their descendants from the earth, their posterity from mankind. Though they plot evil against you and devise wicked schemes, they cannot succeed. You will make them turn their backs when you aim at them with drawn bow. Be exalted in your strength, LORD; we will sing and praise your might.

PSALM 21:1-13

I love to win at games, sports, music competitions, etc. I may be a little bit competitive. Truth be told, most of us love a good victory! This Psalm was written in response to the victory God had given King David and his army in battle. They are rejoicing and praising God for his strength and the success he gave them. The Lord had blessed King David in many ways and given him great favor. However, there is something King David values more than any earthly success or fame. It is found in verses six and seven, "Surely you have granted him unending blessings and made him glad with the joy of your presence. For the king trusts in the LORD; through the unfailing love of the Most High he will not be shaken."

King David found his greatest joy in the presence of the Lord. We find this in Psalm 16:11, "...you will fill me with joy in your presence, with eternal pleasures at your right hand." King David looked forward to being fully in God's presence for eternity.

Because the psalmist found his greatest delight and joy in the Lord, he could put his trust in God's unfailing love and faithfulness. The same can be true for us. If we find our greatest joy in the Lord, then we can trust him fully. This is especially true when we are facing battles.

Although much is made in this Psalm of the victories of the king, it is clear, that the Lord alone gives victory. This Psalm ends the way it began with praise to the Lord for his strength. May we always recognize the source of our success and value him and his presence above all.

Reflection Questions

1. How can our successes give God glory?
2. Do you take more joy in God's presence than in earthly success? If so, how? If not, how can you develop a greater love for his presence?

Father, I look forward to spending eternity fully in your presence. As I learn to find my greatest joy in you now, I put my trust in your unfailing love and faithfulness. I praise you for the strength you give me, and I acknowledge that my successes come from you.

DAY 3 Disc 1 / Track 10

The Good Shepherd

The LORD is my shepherd; I shall not want. He makes me lie down in green pastures. He leads me beside still waters. He restores my soul. He leads me in paths of righteousness for his name's sake. Even though I walk through the valley of the shadow of death, I will fear no evil, for you are with me; your rod and your staff, they comfort me. You prepare a table before me in the presence of my enemies; you anoint my head with oil; my cup overflows. Surely goodness and mercy shall follow me all the days of my life, and I shall dwell in the house of the LORD forever.

PSALM 23:1-6 (ESV)

This is the most famous Psalm as it offers words of peace and comfort to us in our darkest hour. Our Lord, the Good Shepherd, provides all we need like a human shepherd provides for and protects his sheep from danger. In the midst of our chaos, he leads us beside calm waters and restores us.

I remember when I was filled with anxiety and obsessive thoughts, and the Good Shepherd came and gave me peace and restoration. However, in the craziness of life there are many times when I need to again walk "beside still waters" (v. 2-ESV) with the Lord.

Notice that verse three (ESV) says, "He leads me in paths of righteousness for his name's sake." His ultimate goal is to lead us in such a way that we realize his greatness and glorify him. The Lord knows that when we get our eyes off ourselves and our problems, and focus on him, that we can truly be used for his purposes.

Even in our darkest times, we don't have to be afraid because the Lord is with us, protecting and comforting us. A shepherd's staff was an instrument of authority used to count the sheep, guide them along the right paths, and rescue them from danger.[9] I wonder how often we try to figure things out on our own, instead of allowing the Good Shepherd to guide us. His presence removes fear from our lives and he protects us. He also blesses us in unmeasurable ways, even in front of our enemies.

The psalmist enjoyed the protection and help of the Good Shepherd in this life, but ultimately looked forward to being in his presence forever.

Reflection Questions

1. Is there any chaos in your life presently? How can the Good Shepherd help?
2. Has the Good Shepherd provided for you or protected you in a memorable way? If so, how?

Father, you are the Good Shepherd and it is a privilege to be one of your sheep. Thank you for leading me along peaceful paths and protecting me from evil. I choose to trust your protective hand in my life.

DAY 4 Disc 1 / Track 11

The Voice of the Lord

Ascribe to the LORD, you heavenly beings, ascribe to the LORD glory and strength. Ascribe to the LORD the glory due his name; worship the LORD in the splendor of holiness. The voice of the LORD is over the waters; the God of glory thunders, the LORD thunders over the mighty waters. The voice of the LORD is powerful; the voice of the LORD is majestic. The voice of the LORD breaks the cedars; the LORD breaks in pieces the cedars of Lebanon. He makes Lebanon leap like a calf, Sirion like a young wild ox. The voice of the LORD strikes with flashes of lightning. The voice of the LORD shakes the desert; the LORD shakes the Desert of Kadesh. The voice of the LORD twists the oaks and makes the forests bare. And in his temple all cry, "Glory!" The LORD sits enthroned over the flood; the LORD is enthroned as king forever. The LORD gives strength to his people; the LORD blesses his people with peace.

PSALM 29:1-11

This Psalm is a call to all in Heaven and on Earth to give to the Lord the glory of which he is worthy. Verse two says, "Ascribe to the LORD the glory due his name". The Lord is truly worthy of his name. We give him glory as we worship him for who he is and what he has done. It is helpful to have specific things to think about when we sing or talk about the greatness of the Lord. He is the King of Kings and the Lord of Lords (Rev. 19:16) and one day every knee will bow before him (Phil. 2:10).

This Psalm speaks about the Lord's voice and the power it has over creation. His voice rules the waters, splits the forests, and shakes the wilderness. His voice is powerful and full of majesty.

Do we realize the power of God's voice? The Lord is always

speaking. How often are we listening? I believe the Lord also gives us direction in the little things throughout our days. The Holy Spirit encourages us to pray for people, call people, to stop and pay attention to things, and to put others before ourselves.

Verse eleven says, "The LORD gives strength to his people; the Lord blesses his people with peace." If we want his strength, blessing, and peace, then we need to listen to his voice and give him the glory he is due.

Reflection Questions

1. What are some practical ways you can give the Lord the glory due his name?
2. What helps you listen to the Lord's voice?

Lord, you are truly worthy of your name. I honor and glorify you today. I choose to listen and follow your voice today. Help me be attentive to your leading in all things.

DAY 5 Disc 1 / Track 12

Joy Comes in the Morning

I will extol the LORD at all times; his praise will always be on my lips. I will glory in the LORD; let the afflicted hear and I will exalt you, LORD, for you lifted me out of the depths and did not let my enemies gloat over me. LORD my God, I called to you for help, and you healed me. You, Lord, brought me up from the realm of the dead; you spared me from going down to the pit. Sing the praises of the LORD, you his faithful people; praise his holy name. For his anger lasts only a moment, but his favor lasts a lifetime; weeping may stay for the night, but rejoicing comes in the morning. When I felt secure, I said, "I will never be shaken." LORD, when you favored me, you made my royal mountain stand firm; but when you hid your face, I was dismayed. To you, LORD, I called; to the Lord I cried for mercy: "What is gained if I am silenced, if I go down to the pit? Will the dust praise you? Will it proclaim your faithfulness? Hear, LORD, and be merciful to me; LORD, be my help." You turned my wailing into dancing; you removed my sackcloth and clothed me with joy, that my heart may sing your praises and not be silent. LORD my God, I will praise you forever.

PSALM 30:1-12

This Psalm of David was written at the dedication of the temple. God is lifting him up and giving him joy after great difficulty. This temple dedication probably comes from the story in I Chronicles twenty-one and twenty-two.[10] Right before that, King David had taken a census of the nation of Israel. This greatly displeased the Lord and 70,000 Israelites were killed by a plague because of the king's sin.

No wonder there is so much talk about God saving him from the depths, the pit, and turning his tears into rejoicing in this Psalm. I believe this event gave King David a greater understanding of God's mercy.[11] Verse eight says, "To you, LORD, I called; to the Lord I cried for mercy". The Lord could have easily killed King David along with the others. 1 Chronicles 21:17 says, "David said to God, 'Was it not I who ordered the fighting men to be counted? I, the shepherd, have sinned and done wrong. These are but sheep. What have they done? Lord my God, let your hand fall on me and my family, but do not let this plague remain on your people.'"

David truly saw the Lord's anger being short-lived, but his favor lasting forever. He also saw God turning his tears into joy in the morning. Verse eleven says, "You turned my wailing into dancing; you removed my sackcloth and clothed me with joy".

In the Old Testament, we often see God's justice as he punishes his enemies. Mercy is more clearly seen in the New Testament with Jesus dying on the cross for the sins of the world. However, David got to experience mercy in a powerful way when others paid for his sin.

We can take hope from this Psalm knowing that even when we blow it, sin, and make big mistakes that the Lord, in his mercy, will forgive us. In time, joy will truly come in the morning.

Reflection Questions

1. Have you ever done something that caused harm or trouble for others? What happened?
2. How have you experienced God's mercy? Think of a time when he turned your tears into joy.

Lord, thank you for your mercy. Thank you for not giving me what I deserve and for being patient with me. Thank you for turning my sorrow into joy.

DAY 6 Disc 1 / Track 13

Love Beyond Measure

I have a message from God in my heart concerning the sinfulness of the wicked: There is no fear of God before their eyes. In their own eyes they flatter themselves too much to detect or hate their sin. The words of their mouths are wicked and deceitful; they fail to act wisely or do good. Even on their beds they plot evil; they commit themselves to a sinful course and do not reject what is wrong. Your love, LORD, reaches to the heavens, your faithfulness to the skies. Your righteousness is like the highest mountains, your justice like the great deep. You, LORD, preserve both people and animals. How priceless is your unfailing love, O God! People take refuge in the shadow of your wings. They feast on the abundance of your house; you give them drink from your river of delights. For with you is the fountain of life; in your light we see light. Continue your love to those who know you, your righteousness to the upright in heart. May the foot of the proud not come against me, nor the hand of the wicked drive me away. See how the evildoers lie fallen—thrown down, not able to rise!

PSALM 36:1-12

This Psalm distinguishes between wicked people and the love the Lord has for those who follow him. Wicked people have no respect for God, they love themselves, their words are evil, and they're always planning more destruction.

In contrast, the Lord's love "reaches to the heavens" (v. 5). We cannot measure the greatness of his love. His faithfulness reaches to the skies. The Lord is always faithful to his promises. His righteousness is so high it is like Mt. Everest. He is the definition of holiness and his purity towers above all. His justice is "like the great deep" (vs. 6). God's ability to judge justly is beyond our comprehension.

How should we respond to these amazing qualities of our God? They should cause us to worship him with our lives. Verses seven and eight say, "How priceless is your unfailing love, O God! People take refuge in the shadow of your wings. They feast on the abundance of your house; you give them drink from your river of delights."

The proper response to God's love is to run to him in times of need and to value him above all. That is the kind of feasting and drinking the psalmist means. The Lord's "river of delights" (v. 8) is more exquisite, meaningful, and satisfying than anything this world can offer. In order to experience this, we need to spend time reading and meditating on the Word of God, so we come to know how wonderful he truly is.

This week I have been feeling down, bored, and caught in the monotony of my work and baseball games for our boys. I was listening to a sermon this morning by John Piper and as I listened to the message I could sense my spirit being encouraged. He was saying that any sin we struggle with is a competitor against God for our joy.[12] Then I read in this Psalm that the Lord has everything I need for joy and happiness.

Sometimes I fall into the trap of thinking that certain accomplishments or successes will make me happy. I'm reminded again that if I am seeking ultimate happiness in anything other than the Lord I will be disappointed. However, when I seek to find my joy first in him I will experience his joy and love beyond measure.

Reflection Questions

1. How have you experienced the love of the Lord?
2. What sins compete for your joy in life? How can you look to the Lord for joy in those moments?

Lord, your love, faithfulness, righteousness, and justice are amazing. Thank you for loving me! I purpose to fight sin by putting you first in my life. In moments of temptation help me to see your greatness and to drink from your "river of delights" (v. 8).

DAY 7 ⬤ Disc 1 / Track 14

In the Silence

I said, "I will watch my ways and keep my tongue from sin; I will put a muzzle on my mouth while in the presence of the wicked." So I remained utterly silent, not even saying anything good. But my anguish increased; my heart grew hot within me. While I meditated, the fire burned; then I spoke with my tongue: "Show me, LORD, my life's end and the number of my days; let me know how fleeting my life is. You have made my days a mere handbreadth; the span of my years is as nothing before you. Everyone is but a breath, even those who seem secure. Surely everyone goes around like a mere phantom; in vain they rush about, heaping up wealth without knowing whose it will finally be. "But now, Lord, what do I look for? My hope is in you. Save me from all my transgressions; do not make me the scorn of fools. I was silent; I would not open my mouth, for you are the one who has done this. Remove your scourge from me; I am overcome by the blow of your hand. When you rebuke and discipline anyone for their sin, you consume their wealth like a moth—surely everyone is but a breath. "Hear my prayer, LORD, listen to my cry for help; do not be deaf to my weeping. I dwell with you as a foreigner, a stranger, as all my ancestors were. Look away from me, that I may enjoy life again before I depart and am no more."

PSALM 39:1-13

This Psalm has a very serious tone as the writer feels like he is being disciplined by God for some sin. The psalmist chooses to be silent before the wicked. He doesn't want to join in their evil and say something he will regret. However, he gets frustrated and says, "'Show me Lord, my life's end and the number of my days; let me know how fleeting my life is'" (v. 4). He acknowledges that this life is short compared to God's eternal perspective.

People were trying to get ahead and accumulate wealth as if they could keep it forever. This sounds a lot like today. People are desperately trying to keep up with the standard of living of those around them. Unfortunately, many are going into debt and creating bigger problems for themselves.

This reminds me of the theme of the book of Ecclesiastes. The author realizes that the only thing that gives life lasting meaning and direction is following the Lord. Here the psalmist says, "'But now, Lord, what do I look for? My hope is in you'" (v. 7). He realizes that his strength and help for today and for the future can only be found in the Lord.

How do we react when we feel like God is being silent and obstacles are being placed in front of us in life? Do you ever wonder if God might be allowing certain things in our lives to get our attention so we turn from sin, seek him more, etc. I think this Psalm leads us to that conclusion. We are always prone to wander away from the Lord and this is a good reminder to check our heart motivations, and ask the Lord to bring them into harmony with his purposes for us.

This Psalm ends with the author asking the Lord to remove his hand of discipline and bring him back to a place of joy. I believe the Lord will do the same for us in our lives.

Reflection Questions

1. Have you ever felt like God was silent toward you? What happened?
2. What should you do when you feel like obstacles are being placed in front of you in life?

Lord, I want your blessing in my life and I want to hear your voice. When I feel like my plans are being thwarted, I choose to seek and listen to your plans for me.

WEEK

3

DAY 1 Disc 1 / Track 15

The Lord is Pleased With Us

Blessed is the one who considers the poor! In the day of trouble the LORD delivers him; the LORD protects him and keeps him alive; he is called blessed in the land; you do not give him up to the will of his enemies. The LORD sustains him on his sickbed; in his illness you restore him to full health. As for me, I said, "O LORD, be gracious to me; heal me, for I have sinned against you!" My enemies say of me in malice, "When will he die, and his name perish?" And when one comes to see me, he utters empty words, while his heart gathers iniquity; when he goes out, he tells it abroad. All who hate me whisper together about me; they imagine the worst for me. They say, "A deadly thing is poured out on him; he will not rise again from where he lies." Even my close friend in whom I trusted, who ate my bread, has lifted his heel against me. But you, O LORD, be gracious to me, and raise me up, that I may repay them! By this I know that you delight in me: my enemy will not shout in triumph over me. But you have upheld me because of my integrity, and set me in your presence forever. Blessed be the LORD, the God of Israel, from everlasting to everlasting! Amen and Amen.

PSALM 41:1-13

Have you ever had someone close to you betray you? It can be brutally painful. David experienced this more than once. He had played the harp for King Saul, defeated the Philistine giant Goliath for King Saul, and faithfully served in Saul's army. King Saul repaid him by hunting him like a wild animal, trying to kill him.

Later when David was king, his own son Absalom declared himself as king and tried to take David's kingdom from him. I cannot imagine the hurt this caused David.

In this Psalm David begins by saying that the Lord blesses those who look after the weak. The assumption is that he had looked after the weak and is now asking the Lord to help him.[13]

He speaks of being sick and having sinned. Verses seven through nine (ESV) say, "All who hate me whisper together about me; they imagine the worst for me. They say, 'A deadly thing is poured out on him; he will not rise again from where he lies.' Even my close friend in whom I trusted, who ate my bread, has lifted his heel against me."

Even his close friend had turned on him. Jesus used this same phrase when he said, "'He who ate my bread has lifted his heel against me'" (Jn. 13:18-ESV). He was talking about Judas who was going to betray him by turning him over to those who wanted to kill him. If we ever wonder if Jesus knows how we feel when people turn their backs on us, we simply need to remember that one of Jesus' own disciple's betrayal led to his death.

Then David asks for the Lord's help in dealing with his enemies-showing that the Lord delighted in and was pleased with David. We know that the Lord loves and is pleased with his children. Zephaniah 3:17 says, "'He will take great delight in you; in his love he will no longer rebuke you, but will rejoice over you with singing.'"

What an amazing promise that the Lord is so pleased with us that he takes joy in singing over us! There have been many love songs written over the years, but I am sure the Creator's songs are infinitely better than ours. I am looking forward to hearing them in Heaven. Rather than striving to please God today let's rest in his love for us.

Reflection Questions
1. How could David keep trusting the Lord when those close to him betrayed him?
2. How can knowing God is pleased with you affect every area of your life?

Father, thank you for loving me. When people let me down, I know I can always count on you. I choose to walk in confidence today knowing that you are pleased with me and love to sing over me.

DAY 2 🔘 Disc 1 / Track 16

My Joy and my Delight

Vindicate me, my God, and plead my cause against an unfaithful nation. Rescue me from those who are deceitful and wicked. You are God my stronghold. Why have you rejected me? Why must I go about mourning, oppressed by the enemy? Send me your light and your faithful care, let them lead me; let them bring me to your holy mountain, to the place where you dwell. Then I will go to the altar of God, to God, my joy and my delight. I will praise you with the lyre, O God, my God. Why, my soul, are you downcast? Why so disturbed within me? Put your hope in God, for I will yet praise him, my Savior and my God.

PSALM 43:1-5

Who do you love to be around? We usually look forward to spending time with those who encourage us, make us laugh, or invest in us in some way.

Like Psalm forty-two, this Psalm is a call back to God's presence. The psalmist is crying out for help from his enemies, he is feeling rejected by God, and he is in distress.

Verse three says, "Send me your light and your faithful care, let them lead me; let them bring me to your holy mountain, to the place where you dwell." He is asking to be led back to the presence of the Lord. He knows that God's presence is where he will find strength, peace, and joy. He calls the Lord his joy and his delight.

There are some people who I make it a habit to regularly go to coffee with, meet up for lunch, etc. I find that these appointments take on greater significance and meaning when life is difficult. In those times, I look to those people for encouragement, advice, prayer, and support. Sometimes I forget how much I need these relationships and the joy they bring me.

In a much greater and profound way, we desperately need to be in the presence of the Lord-especially when times are tough. Any quality or trait we appreciate in someone has its origin in God. He possesses all of those qualities! As the psalmist was called back to God's presence, so we are called to spend time with the Lord for encouragement, direction, and to exalt him.

Like the psalmist worshiped with the lyre, I love to worship the Lord with instruments like the piano or guitar. I'm always amazed and grateful at how my distresses diminish when I worship the Lord. It is often a matter of perspective. My troubles seem smaller in light of God's greatness and power.

Reflection Questions

1. Think of three people you love to be around. What quality in them stands out most to you?

2. How should knowing the Lord possesses all of these qualities change us?

Lord, you are my joy and my delight. When I forget just how much I need you, let my earthly relationships be a pointer to you and an encouragement to seek your presence.

The City of God

Great is the LORD, and most worthy of praise, in the city of our God, his holy mountain. Beautiful in its loftiness, the joy of the whole earth, like the heights of Zaphon is Mount Zion, the city of the Great King. God is in her citadels; he has shown himself to be her fortress. When the kings joined forces, when they advanced together, they saw her and were astounded; they fled in terror. Trembling seized them there, pain like that of a woman in labor. You destroyed them like ships of Tarshish shattered by an east wind. As we have heard, so we have seen in the city of the LORD Almighty, in the city of our God: God makes her secure forever. Within your temple, O God, we meditate on your unfailing love. Like your name, O God, your praise reaches to the ends of the earth; your right hand is filled with righteousness. Mount Zion rejoices, the villages of Judah are glad because of your judgments. Walk about Zion, go around her, count her towers, consider well her ramparts, view her citadels, that you may tell of them to the next generation. For this God is our God for ever and ever; he will be our guide even to the end.

PSALM 48:1-14

This Psalm of praise focuses on the city of Jerusalem. Why was this city called "the joy of the whole earth" (v. 2)? It was the Israelites' place of worship as the temple was located there. The Lord's presence was in Jerusalem, and he protected it from foreign armies. It says they ran away! Most importantly, we know that Jesus was later crucified right outside Jerusalem. This was the place where our Savior died to forgive our sins and give us new life. It has great spiritual significance.

Verses nine and ten say, "Within your temple, O God, we meditate on your unfailing love. Like your name, O God, your praise reaches to the ends of the earth". When we are in God's presence, we think about his love for us. Just as God's character and fame have spread around the world, so do his praises! The more we learn about the Lord from the Bible regarding his character and what he has done, it makes us want to worship him. When I see him at work in my life and in the lives of others around me, I cannot help but sing his praises.

The end of this Psalm speaks of telling the next generation about God's great exploits and then it says, "For this God is our God for ever and ever; he will be our guide even to the end" (v. 14). Just as the Lord was faithful to Jerusalem, he will be faithful to his children forever. What an amazing promise!

If we ever wonder if God is watching over us and protecting us, then we simply need to look at his watchful hand over Jerusalem and the people of Israel throughout the years.

Reflection Questions

1. What is significant to you about the Lord's relationship to Jerusalem and the people of Israel?
2. If God is our guide "to the end" (v. 14), how should that change our outlook on life?

Father, I see how you have been faithful to your people over the years. I take confidence in the promise that you will lead and guide me today and forever. I choose to declare your praises to those around me today!

DAY 4 ● Disc 1 / Track 18

My Treasure

Hear this, all you peoples; listen, all who live in this world, both low and high, rich and poor alike: My mouth will speak words of wisdom; the meditation of my heart will give you understanding. I will turn my ear to a proverb; with the harp I will expound my riddle: Why should I fear when evil days come, when wicked deceivers surround me—those who trust in their wealth and boast of their great riches? No one can redeem the life of another or give to God a ransom for them— the ransom for a life is costly, no payment is ever enough—so that they should live on forever and not see decay. For all can see that the wise die, that the foolish and the senseless also perish, leaving their wealth to others. Their tombs will remain their houses forever, their dwellings for endless generations, though they had named lands after themselves. People, despite their wealth, do not endure; they are like the beasts that perish. This is the fate of those who trust in themselves, and of their followers, who approve their sayings. They are like sheep and are destined to die; death will be their shepherd (but the upright will prevail over them in the morning). Their forms will decay in the grave, far from their princely mansions. But God will redeem me from the realm of the dead; he will surely take me to himself.

PSALM 49:1-15

It is amazing to me how much emphasis our society puts on wealth today. In many ways riches equate to power in our culture. This was no different in the day when this Psalm was written, however the psalmist reminds us of the fleeting nature of wealth.

A message is given to the rich and the poor. Why should we fear when we are surrounded by people who put their trust in money? That's where those people find their significance. In light of eternity, financial status is meaningless. No amount of money can assure anyone a spot in Heaven.

Verses seven through nine say, "No one can redeem the life of another or give to God a ransom for them— the ransom for a life is costly, no payment is ever enough—so that they should live on forever and not see decay." We will all die one day and we cannot take anything with us. The things we leave behind on this earth will surely go to others.

What is the point being made? Those who trust in wealth are actually trusting in themselves. Managing our money well is a wise and needed endeavor for this life, but the hope given in this Psalm has to do with the life to come.

"But God will redeem me from the realm of the dead; he will surely take me to himself" (v. 15). The hope for those who trust in the Lord instead of their money is a future with the Lord forever. Only Jesus can forgive our sins and give us the gift of Heaven. It really comes down to what we value most. Jesus said, "For where your treasure is there your heart will be also" (Matt. 6:21).

When we look at our lives and how we spend our time, we can see what is most important to us. What are we treasuring? When the Lord has our heart, not only is our future secure, but our days are filled with the joy that comes from delighting in Him.

Reflection Questions

1. Do you feel pressure to live up to a certain standard financially? If so, how does that affect you?

2. How does making Jesus your treasure change your outlook on wealth or financial status?

Lord, I am grateful for the financial blessings you have given me. Thank you for the reminder that treasuring you first in this life has eternal significance.

DAY 5 Disc 1 / Track 19

Hope in Your Name

Why do you boast of evil, you mighty hero? Why do you boast all day long, you who are a disgrace in the eyes of God? You who practice deceit, your tongue plots destruction; it is like a sharpened razor. You love evil rather than good, falsehood rather than speaking the truth. You love every harmful word, you deceitful tongue! Surely God will bring you down to everlasting ruin: He will snatch you up and pluck you from your tent; he will uproot you from the land of the living. The righteous will see and fear; they will laugh at you, saying, "Here now is the man who did not make God his stronghold but trusted in his great wealth and grew strong by destroying others!" But I am like an olive tree flourishing in the house of God; I trust in God's unfailing love for ever and ever. For what you have done I will always praise you in the presence of your faithful people. And I will hope in your name, for your name is good.

PSALM 52:1-9

The backstory of this Psalm is that David is on the run from King Saul who wants to kill him. David stops in to see Ahimelek the priest who gives him and his soldiers some bread and he prays for them. One of Saul's servants, Doeg the Edomite was there and overheard the whole encounter. Doeg tells Saul that Ahimelek helped David, and Saul kills Ahimelek and the entire town of Nob where he was from. One of Ahimelek's sons escapes to tell David the news. David feels responsible for the death of Ahimelek's family (1 Sam. 21-22).

In light of these events, this Psalm describes those who do evil and then brag about it. They are liars who love their evil ways. David talks about the judgement that God will bring their way. He was probably thinking about Doeg and what he had done.[14] David says that the godly will actually laugh at those who trust in their wealth and destroy others, instead of following the Lord.

David contrasts this with the righteous. He says, "But I am like an olive tree flourishing in the house of God; I trust in God's unfailing love for ever and ever. For what you have done I will always praise you in the presence of your faithful people. And I will hope in your name, for your name is good" (vv. 8-9).

Olive trees live for hundreds of years or more. This Psalm says the righteous will be successful, and like an olive tree, will outlast those who don't follow the Lord. The righteous trust in God's love and focus on praising him for what he has done. Putting our hope in God's name is staking our foundation on who he is and what he has done. This is a firm foundation that will not disappoint us today or in the future. If people do things to harm us or those around us we need to remember that the Lord looks out for his people. Proverbs 18:10 says, "The name of the LORD is a strong tower; the righteous man runs into it and is safe."

Reflection Questions

1. Have you ever had someone do something nice for you, and they paid a price for it later? If so, how did you feel?
2. Do you believe that God's protection for his people is stronger than the plans of the wicked? If so, how should this affect you?

Lord, my hope is in your name. When evil people threaten my sense of well-being, I choose to trust in you. You are my protector and you are faithful.

DAY 6   Disc 1 / Track 20

Cast Your Cares on Him

Listen to my prayer, O God, do not ignore my plea; hear me and answer me. My thoughts trouble me and I am distraught because of what my enemy is saying, because of the threats of the wicked; for they bring down suffering on me and assail me in their anger. My heart is in anguish within me; the terrors of death have fallen on me. Fear and trembling have beset me; horror has overwhelmed me. I said, "Oh, that I had the wings of a dove! I would fly away and be at rest. I would flee far away and stay in the desert; I would hurry to my place of shelter, far from the tempest and storm." Lord, confuse the wicked, confound their words, for I see violence and strife in the city. Day and night they prowl about on its walls; malice and abuse are within it. Destructive forces are at work in the city; threats and lies never leave its streets. If an enemy were insulting me, I could endure it; if a foe were rising against me, I could hide. But it is you, a man like myself, my companion, my close friend, with whom I once enjoyed sweet fellowship at the house of God, as we walked about among the worshipers. Let death take my enemies by surprise; let them go down alive to the realm of the dead, for evil finds lodging among them. As for me, I call to God, and the Lord saves me. Evening, morning and noon I cry out in distress, and he hears my voice. He rescues me unharmed from the battle waged against me, even though many oppose me. God, who is enthroned from of old, who does not change—he will hear them and humble them, because they have no fear of God. My companion attacks his friends; he violates his covenant. His talk is smooth as butter, yet war is in his heart; his words are more soothing than oil, yet they are drawn swords. Cast your cares on the Lord and he will sustain you; he will never let the righteous be shaken. But you, God, will bring down the wicked into the pit of decay; the bloodthirsty and deceitful will not live out half their days. But as for me, I trust in you.

PSALM 55:1-23

This is a heart-wrenching Psalm because it describes David's struggle when a close friend turns on him. The person was someone with whom David worshiped and enjoyed "sweet fellowship" (v.14). It is extremely painful when someone we love dearly, hurts us.

He begins the Psalm by crying out to the Lord for help in light of what his friend is saying. He says, "My heart is in anguish within me; the terrors of death have fallen on me. Fear and trembling have beset me; horror has overwhelmed me (vv. 4-5). David is in a bad place and his suffering has seemingly consumed him.

I have noticed my tendency to become consumed with things that are troubling me or causing me anxiety. David probably experienced that too, and his troubles were more challenging than most of ours.

However, notice where David chooses to focus. He says that he cries out to God all day long, who hears him and saves him. Then he talks about his friend who is hurting him again. Isn't that how we are? Even in our crying out to God, we tend to get sidetracked and focus again on our problems.

Then David says, "Cast your cares on the Lord and he will sustain you; he will never let the righteous be shaken... But as for me, I trust in you" (vv. 22-23b).

David tells himself and his listeners to give their pain, worry, and cares to God knowing that only the Lord can help them. I too have to tell myself to give those things to the Lord. It is often a struggle, but when I cast my cares on him, I don't have to carry them anymore. It's a liberating feeling. I Peter 5:7 says, "Cast all your anxiety on him because he cares for you." We can do this because he loves us. David ends this Psalm by affirming his trust in the Lord.

Reflection Questions

1. How can you focus on God's promises when anxieties are overwhelming you?
2. How do you know when you have left your cares in God's hands?

Lord, I cast my cares on you today. I choose to focus on your promises instead of the challenges, worries, and concerns I see around me today.

DAY 7   ● Disc 1 / Track 21

Trust in the Lord

Be merciful to me, my God, for my enemies are in hot pursuit; all day long they press their attack. My adversaries pursue me all day long; in their pride many are attacking me. When I am afraid, I put my trust in you. In God, whose word I praise—in God I trust and am not afraid. What can mere mortals do to me? All day long they twist my words; all their schemes are for my ruin. They conspire, they lurk, they watch my steps, hoping to take my life. Because of their wickedness do not let them escape; in your anger, God, bring the nations down. Record my misery; list my tears on your scroll—are they not in your record? Then my enemies will turn back when I call for help. By this I will know that God is for me. In God, whose word I praise, in the LORD, whose word I praise—in God I trust and am not afraid. What can man do to me? I am under vows to you, my God; I will present my thank offerings to you. For you have delivered me from death and my feet from stumbling, that I may walk before God in the light of life.

PSALM 56:1-13

How do you respond to fear? Do you boldly face your fears, check everything out and then proceed, or timidly move forward? We all respond to fear differently and yet fear can be paralyzing in our lives if we don't deal with it appropriately.

We are told that the Philistines had seized David when this Psalm was written. They were his enemies and he probably had every reason to be afraid. David says, "When I am afraid, I put my trust in you. In God, whose word I praise—in God I trust and am not afraid. What can mere mortals do to me?" (vv. 3-4).

David knew what to do when fear came knocking at his door-trust in the Lord. David knew that ultimate power and authority was not in the hands of the Philistines but in the hands of his God. He was able to praise God's Word because the Lord had been faithful to him and to the nation of Israel in the past. He trusted that God would be faithful in the future as well.

This is a great lesson for us today. What fears have you been dealing with? I am sometimes afraid to speak up when I know I should. There are times when I am afraid to do something because I don't want to be judged or laughed at. When we compare man's power to God's, we realize that there truly is no reason to fear. We can and should trust him at all times.

Verses eight and nine say, "Record my misery; list my tears on your scroll—are they not in your record? Then my enemies will turn back when I call for help. By this I will know that God is for me." David talks about the Lord keeping track of all his tears. The idea is that if God keeps a record of all his tears, then he will be faithful to help David in his time of need.[15]

The Lord will help us in our time of need as well. Just this week I was comparing myself to someone else wishing I had the opportunities and talents they had. In reality, I was dealing with jealousy that was fueled by the fear of being insignificant.

Like David, I am choosing to trust instead of giving in to fear. My life is in the Lord's hands. Rather than comparing myself to others, to the best of my ability, I choose to glorify him with everything he has given me.

Reflection Questions

1. How can we trust the Lord when we are tempted to fear?
2. Have you ever been afraid of something that God later delivered you from? What happened?

Lord, I am so thankful that I can trust you with my fears. I choose to value your Word above the words of man. You hold the ultimate power and authority. I praise you for your Word!

WEEK

4

DAY 1 ● Disc 1 / Track 22

Refresh me Lord

Hear my cry, O God; listen to my prayer. From the ends of the earth I call to you, I call as my heart grows faint; lead me to the rock that is higher than I. For you have been my refuge, a strong tower against the foe. I long to dwell in your tent forever and take refuge in the shelter of your wings. For you, God, have heard my vows; you have given me the heritage of those who fear your name. Increase the days of the king's life, his years for many generations. May he be enthroned in God's presence forever; appoint your love and faithfulness to protect him. Then I will ever sing in praise of your name and fulfill my vows day after day.

PSALM 61:1-8

Who do you call on when you grow weary? In this Psalm David says that his "heart grows faint" (v. 1). I have felt that way many times. My first reaction is sometimes to seek out something to distract me, like a good movie, concert, or a vacation. Other times I seek encouragement from people when I need refreshing. This Psalm reminds us that there is ultimately only one place we can go for lasting strength, protection, and peace-to the Lord.

Verse two says, "lead me to the rock that is higher than I." The Lord is greater and more powerful than we are. He can certainly provide for us and refresh us in times of need.

I think we forget how powerful the Lord is. Like Moses at the burning bush, we get so focused on our inadequacies that we lack confidence in the Lord. The Lord told him that he was the man to lead the people of Israel out of Egypt, and Moses was sure God had chosen the wrong person (Ex. 3). In other words, we don't take God at his word because we are too focused on our perceived weaknesses.

David says that the Lord is his protection and that he longs to be in his presence forever. He also talks about the "...heritage of those who fear your name" (v. 5). There are blessings both here and in eternity for those who love, honor, and respect the Lord above everything else.

Then David asks for God's faithfulness and love to be his protection. He says he will respond in praise and obedience to the Lord for protecting him. How often does the Lord answer our prayers and then we forget to thank him? When the Lord protects and refreshes us, he wants us to continually be drawing closer to him as our trust in him grows. Let's make sure we express our gratitude to him today!

Reflection Questions
1. What refreshes you when you are weary?
2. What habits or practices direct your focus from self to the Lord?

Lord, I turn to you for refreshment knowing true renewal comes from you. I choose to embrace the tasks, mission, and life to which you have called me. Forgive me for looking at my weaknesses when I should be focusing on you.

Creation Praises You

Praise awaits you, our God, in Zion; to you our vows will be fulfilled. You who answer prayer, to you all people will come. When we were overwhelmed by sins, you forgave our transgressions. Blessed are those you choose and bring near to live in your courts! We are filled with the good things of your house, of your holy temple. You answer us with awesome and righteous deeds, God our Savior, the hope of all the ends of the earth and of the farthest seas, who formed the mountains by your power, having armed yourself with strength, who stilled the roaring of the seas, the roaring of their waves, and the turmoil of the nations. The whole earth is filled with awe at your wonders; where morning dawns, where evening fades, you call forth songs of joy. You care for the land and water it; you enrich it abundantly. The streams of God are filled with water to provide the people with grain, for so you have ordained it. You drench its furrows and level its ridges; you soften it with showers and bless its crops. You crown the year with your bounty, and your carts overflow with abundance. The grasslands of the wilderness overflow; the hills are clothed with gladness. The meadows are covered with flocks and the valleys are mantled with grain; they shout for joy and sing.

PSALM 65:1-13

Do you ever get caught up in the wonder and beauty of God's creation? Living in the Pacific Northwest, I am well aware of the beautiful mountains, Puget Sound, and islands all around us. These things can point us to the greatness of the one who made them.

This Psalm focuses on the Lord's provision for the earth he has made and how creation declares his praises. It kicks off stating that praise awaits God. Like a servant waits for his master, praise waits for God.[16] It speaks of everyone coming to the Lord because he answers prayer. Basically, anyone who is wise will seek the Lord in prayer. It says he is the only one who can forgive our sins.

Then it says, "Blessed are those you choose and bring near to live in your courts" (v. 4). The word "blessed" here means "happy". Those who are in close relationship with the Lord are happy. Are you wanting God's blessing and joy in your life? Then draw near to him and seek his presence daily through worship, prayer, and studying his Word.

Verse eight says, "The whole earth is filled with awe at your wonders; where morning dawns, where evening fades, you call forth songs of joy." What an amazing statement! The Lord is calling forth joyful songs from his creation to worship him. When we wake up in the morning, God is calling us to exalt him. I got up at 6:15am this morning and took one of our sons to swim team right away. To be honest, we had a stressful morning and God's praise wasn't on my tongue. I was frustrated and upset. However, I could've been singing a song of praise to the Lord. In the evening, his song should be on our lips as well.

Let's allow God's physical creation all around us to remind us to give him glory today!

Reflection Questions

1. What do you enjoy most about God's physical creation?
2. How can creation enlarge our view of the Lord?

Father, I am grateful for your beautiful creation all around me. I am amazed at the intricacies of everything you have made. I worship you in response to this amazing world you have created!

DAY 3 ● Disc 2 / Track 1

Make His Praise Glorious

Shout for joy to God, all the earth! Sing the glory of his name; make his praise glorious. Say to God, "How awesome are your deeds! So great is your power that your enemies cringe before you. All the earth bows down to you; they sing praise to you, they sing the praises of your name." Come and see what God has done, his awesome deeds for mankind! He turned the sea into dry land, they passed through the waters on foot-come, let us rejoice in him. He rules forever by his power, his eyes watch the nations-let not the rebellious rise up against him. Praise our God, all peoples, let the sound of his praise be heard; he has preserved our lives and kept our feet from slipping.

PSALM 66:1-9

As a worship pastor, a large portion of my week is spent preparing for a half hour of corporate worship on Sunday. I choose the songs, prepare the music for rehearsal, rehearse with the team, and then practice again before Sunday. This is done because we want to offer our very best to God in worship, in honor of his greatness. Secondarily, we want to lead others into his presence in the most engaging way possible. He is worthy of the very best we have to give!

This Psalm says it like this, "Sing the glory of his name; make his praise glorious. Say to God, 'How awesome are your deeds! So great is your power that your enemies cringe before you'" (vv. 2-3). Making his praise glorious is bringing our best offering of worship to the Lord because of his glory, power, and deeds.[17]

In my freshman year of college, I played a piece by Bach for a piano recital and it didn't go well. The other performers played much better than I did. My nerves got the best of me and my memory was faulty. I was embarrassed! After the fact, I realized that my practice and preparation needed to improve. From then on, I was much more meticulous and careful in my preparation for recitals because I wanted to do my best.

In the same way, the Lord deserves the best we can give him with our lives in worship and praise to him. This Psalm recalls the way he parted the waters for his people to escape from the Egyptians, and he watches over and protects us today as well.

Offering our best to the Lord affects our thoughts, attitudes, speech, and relationships. We realize that those things are outward reflections of what is happening in our hearts. If our heart's desire is to make Jesus look glorious in all we do, then we treat others differently because of our desire to please him. We can show grace, love, and kindness to people even when they don't deserve it. That is exactly what Jesus offers to us by his death on the cross. "But God demonstrates his own love for us in this: While we were still sinners, Christ died for us" (Rom. 5:8).

Reflection Questions
1. Have you ever done your best on a project or task? What Happened?
2. How can you offer your best to the Lord at home, work, and church?

Jesus, thank you for dying on the cross so my sins can be forgiven. I offer my life to you today in honor of your glory and greatness. I choose to make your praise glorious by offering my best worship to you today!

DAY 4 ● Disc 2 / Track 2

Zeal for Your House

Save me, O God, for the waters have come up to my neck. I sink in the miry depths where there is no foothold. I have come into the deep waters; the floods engulf me. I am worn out calling for help; my throat is parched. My eyes fail, looking for my God. Those who hate me without reason outnumber the hairs of my head; many are my enemies without cause, those who seek to destroy me. I am forced to restore what I did not steal. You, God, know my folly; my guilt is not hidden from you. Lord, the LORD Almighty, may those who hope in you not be disgraced because of me; God of Israel, may those who seek you not be put to shame because of me. For I endure scorn for your sake, and shame covers my face. I am a foreigner to my own family, a stranger to my own mother's children; for zeal for your house consumes me, and the insults of those who insult you fall on me. When I weep and fast, I must endure scorn; when I put on sackcloth, people make sport of me. Those who sit at the gate mock me, and I am the song of the drunkards. But I pray to you, LORD, in the time of your favor; in your great love, O God, answer me with your sure salvation. Rescue me from the mire, do not let me sink; deliver me from those who hate me, from the deep waters. Do not let the floodwaters engulf me or the depths swallow me up or the pit close its mouth over me. Answer me, LORD, out of the goodness of your love; in your great mercy turn to me. Do not hide your face from your servant; answer me quickly, for I am in trouble. Come near and rescue me; deliver me because of my foes.

PSALM 69:1-18

Have you ever been in a situation where you were surrounded by troubles and you felt like you were drowning in them? It can be manageable when troubles come in one area of our lives, but when, for instance, we are experiencing troubles at home and work simultaneously, it can be overwhelming. This is the second most quoted Psalm in the New Testament, and it is viewed as a foreshadowing of Jesus' sufferings.[18]

In this Psalm, David is calling out for the Lord to save him and he is exhausted from it. He is looking for God but cannot find him. Do you ever feel like that? I often feel like God is far off when I am focused on my problems. It is a matter of perspective. However, I have found that when the Lord doesn't immediately take my difficulties away, he wants to walk with me through them.

David had many enemies who hated him, but he also acknowledges his own sin in this Psalm. Sometimes our challenges are due to other people or circumstances, and other times they are because of our own choices.

Verses six and seven say, "Lord, the Lord Almighty, may those who hope in you not be disgraced because of me; God of Israel, may those who seek you not be put to shame because of me. For I endure scorn for your sake, and shame covers my face."

David asks the Lord to not let harm come to others as a result of his own mistakes because he endures trouble for the Lord's sake. Then he says, "for zeal for your house consumes me, and the insults of those who insult you fall on me" (v. 9). David was so passionate about living for the Lord, being in his presence, and serving him, that he was willing to be persecuted. Today in our society, some treat spiritual things with a "take it or leave it" attitude, but we need the passionate heart David had. He loved the Lord so much that he was willing to be persecuted for his sake.

Then he calls on God to answer him and rescue him because of the Lord's great love. People made fun of David and hated him, but he turned to the Lord for help and deliverance. What an example for us! Rather than complaining and feeling sorry for ourselves, let's turn to the Lord in our time of greatest need because of his great love for us.

Reflection Questions

1. Have you ever experienced trouble in multiple areas of life simultaneously? What did you do?
2. Does zeal for God's house consume you? How can that aid in times of persecution?

Father, help me when I feel overwhelmed with the circumstances around me. I call out to you for help. Like David, I want "zeal for your house" (v. 9) to consume me and sustain me in times of persecution.

DAY 5   Disc 2 / Track 3

Build my Faith

I cried out to God for help; I cried out to God to hear me. When I was in distress, I sought the Lord; at night I stretched out untiring hands, and I would not be comforted. I remembered you, God, and I groaned; I meditated, and my spirit grew faint. You kept my eyes from closing; I was too troubled to speak. I thought about the former days, the years of long ago; I remembered my songs in the night. My heart meditated and my spirit asked: "Will the Lord reject forever? Will he never show his favor again? Has his unfailing love vanished forever? Has his promise failed for all time? Has God forgotten to be merciful? Has he in anger withheld his compassion?" Then I thought, "To this I will appeal: the years when the Most High stretched out his right hand. I will remember the deeds of the LORD; yes, I will remember your miracles of long ago. I will consider all your works and meditate on all your mighty deeds." Your ways, God, are holy. What god is as great as our God? You are the God who performs miracles; you display your power among the peoples. With your mighty arm you redeemed your people, the descendants of Jacob and Joseph. The waters saw you, God, the waters saw you and writhed; the very depths were convulsed. The clouds poured down water, the heavens resounded with thunder; your arrows flashed back and forth. Your thunder was heard in the whirlwind, your lightning lit up the world; the earth trembled and quaked. Your path led through the sea, your way through the mighty waters, though your footprints were not seen. You led your people like a flock by the hand of Moses and Aaron.

PSALM 77:1-20

Have you ever been so distressed about something that it consumed you? You thought about it during the day and it kept you up at night as well. Here the psalmist Asaph is crying out to God for help in his trouble. Not only is he losing sleep, but he is so upset he can't even talk about it.

He does remember God's faithfulness to him in the past. But he is still at a point of frustration when he says, "'Will the Lord reject forever? Will he never show his favor again?'" (v. 7). When we are struggling, it can be hard to put our faith in the Lord's favor, love, mercy, and compassion because we cannot see them at work. That is where faith comes in. Heb. 11:1 says, "Now faith is confidence in what we hope for and assurance about what we do not see." Faith is believing what we know to be true about God from his Word even when we cannot see it.

Asaph begins to recall the specific miracles the Lord did for the children of Israel (like leading them through the Red Sea on dry ground) and he meditates on them. He becomes so overwhelmed with God's holiness and greatness that he says, "What god is as great as our God?" (v. 13). What an amazing change-he went from utter discouragement to faith! When we begin to think about and ponder God's faithfulness to people in the Bible, to those around us, and in our own lives, it builds our faith.

When I recall how anxious and troubled I used to be, and how God has brought me to such a greater place of peace and rest in my life, all I can do is worship him. Just recalling this builds my faith in the midst of my current difficulties.

No matter what we are facing today, let's allow the Lord to build our faith in the present by remembering his great works in the past.

Reflection Questions

1. How do you respond when you are distressed, and God doesn't seem to hear your prayers?
2. Can you recall a time when the Lord came through for you? How does that encourage you today?

Lord, when I am discouraged I choose to remember the amazing things you have done in the past. I put my faith in your promises knowing that you love me.

DAY 6 Disc 2 / Track 4

Restore Me

You, LORD, showed favor to your land; you restored the fortunes of Jacob. You forgave the iniquity of your people and covered all their sins. You set aside all your wrath and turned from your fierce anger. Restore us again, God our Savior, and put away your displeasure toward us. Will you be angry with us forever? Will you prolong your anger through all generations? Will you not revive us again, that your people may rejoice in you? Show us your unfailing love, LORD, and grant us your salvation. I will listen to what God the LORD says; he promises peace to his people, his faithful servants—but let them not turn to folly. Surely his salvation is near those who fear him, that his glory may dwell in our land. Love and faithfulness meet together; righteousness and peace kiss each other. Faithfulness springs forth from the earth, and righteousness looks down from heaven. The LORD will indeed give what is good, and our land will yield its harvest. Righteousness goes before him and prepares the way for his steps.

PSALM 85:1-13

This Psalm recalls how the Lord forgave Israel's sin in the past letting go of his anger and blessing them. The psalmist is asking God to restore them again and to put his anger away. Then he says, "Will you not revive us again, that your people may rejoice in you?" (v. 6).

Have you ever done something wrong and felt so horrible about it that it affected your joy? As a kid, I remember saying something horribly mean to someone about their physical appearance. I got into big trouble for it. The ironic part about that story is that my comment was so untrue. When I've done something wrong like that and then asked for forgiveness, having the relationship restored is wonderful. In the same way, when the Lord restores us, our joy returns.

The psalmist asks for the Lord to show his love and to save them. Verse eight refers to a message from the Lord that may have come from a priest.[19] This message promised peace to those who were faithful to the Lord. The same is true for us today.

Verse nine says, "Surely his salvation is near those who fear him, that his glory may dwell in our land." How can we know that God will deliver us in our times of need? We cultivate a heart attitude of respect and fear of the Lord that results in God's greatness and glory being seen to those around us.

Reflection Questions

1. Have you ever had a relationship restored? What happened?
2. Have you ever been restored to the Lord? Did you experience joy?

Lord, thank you that when I sin you are willing to forgive me and restore me to a place of peace and joy in my walk with you. I choose to keep short accounts with others so that I can experience peace in those relationships as well.

DAY 7 Disc 2 / Track 5

Our Amazing God

I will sing of the LORD's great love forever; with my mouth I will make your faithfulness known through all generations. I will declare that your love stands firm forever, that you have established your faithfulness in heaven itself. You said, "I have made a covenant with my chosen one, I have sworn to David my servant, 'I will establish your line forever and make your throne firm through all generations.'" The heavens praise your wonders, LORD, your faithfulness too, in the assembly of the holy ones. For who in the skies above can compare with the LORD? Who is like the LORD among the heavenly beings? In the council of the holy ones God is greatly feared; he is more awesome than all who surround him. Who is like you, LORD God Almighty? You, LORD, are mighty, and your faithfulness surrounds you. You rule over the surging sea; when its waves mount up, you still them. You crushed Rahab like one of the slain; with your strong arm you scattered your enemies. The heavens are yours, and yours also the earth; you founded the world and all that is in it. You created the north and the south; Tabor and Hermon sing for joy at your name. Your arm is endowed with power; your hand is strong, your right hand exalted. Righteousness and justice are the foundation of your throne; love and faithfulness go before you. Blessed are those who have learned to acclaim you, who walk in the light of your presence, Lord. They rejoice in your name all day long; they celebrate your righteousness. For you are their glory and strength, and by your favor you exalt our horn.

PSALM 89:1-17

There is something powerful that happens when we sing about God's faithful love to us. We know that we don't deserve his love because of our shortcomings, but this Psalm reminds us that he will never stop loving us. When we proclaim the Lord's faithfulness to all the generations, we encourage them to trust him with their lives as well. I love to tell stories to our three boys about the faithfulness of the Lord, because it builds their faith.

Verses five and six say, "The heavens praise your wonders, Lord, your faithfulness too, in the assembly of the holy ones. For who in the skies above can compare with the Lord?" The Lord's amazing works and faithfulness are declared in the heavens and we should worship him for those things on the earth as well. It says that there is no one like the Lord. He is amazing and powerful and faithfulness surrounds him. When we get an understanding of his greatness, we will never be the same. We realize that nothing else compares to him.

Lately I have been reading some short biographies of great fathers of the faith. They had such an amazing view of God, that it led them to do great things for God. The same will be true in our lives as well. For instance, Martin Luther was a professor at the University of Wittenberg, wrote numerous theological works, translated the Bible into German, and preached regularly to a congregation.[20] Like Luther, when we understand who we serve, we will strive to accomplish great things for his glory.

The psalmist goes on to say, "Blessed are those who have learned to acclaim you, who walk in the light of your presence, Lord. They rejoice in your name all day long" (vv. 15-16).

This says that the way to be happy in life is to learn to worship the Lord and to live with the light of his presence shining on us. What a great word picture! I desperately need the light of God's presence shining on me. In other words, we seek his presence and follow after his ways. Those people have joy in the Lord all day long as the Lord is their focus and strength. They are delighting in the Lord!

Reflection Questions

1. Do you have personal stories of the Lord's faithfulness to you? Think about one.

2. Have you experienced the joy that comes from learning to worship him? If so, what difference does it make in your life?

Lord, I am so thankful for your love and faithfulness to me. I know that the key to joy in life is learning to exalt your greatness and following in your ways.

WEEK

5

DAY 1   Disc 2 / Track 6

Teach us to Number our Days

Lord, you have been our dwelling place throughout all generations. Before the mountains were born or you brought forth the whole world, from everlasting to everlasting you are God. You turn people back to dust, saying, "Return to dust, you mortals." A thousand years in your sight are like a day that has just gone by, or like a watch in the night. Yet you sweep people away in the sleep of death—they are like the new grass of the morning: In the morning it springs up new, but by evening it is dry and withered. We are consumed by your anger and terrified by your indignation. You have set our iniquities before you, our secret sins in the light of your presence. All our days pass away under your wrath; we finish our years with a moan. Our days may come to seventy years, or eighty, if our strength endures; yet the best of them are but trouble and sorrow, for they quickly pass, and we fly away. If only we knew the power of your anger! Your wrath is as great as the fear that is your due. Teach us to number our days, that we may gain a heart of wisdom. Relent, LORD! How long will it be? Have compassion on your servants. Satisfy us in the morning with your unfailing love, that we may sing for joy and be glad all our days.

PSALM 90:1-14

How closely do you monitor how you spend your time? Many of us have read books or taken classes on time management and there are definite benefits to using our time wisely. However, it seems if we micromanage every minute, it can take some of the joy and spontaneity out of life.

Moses wrote this Psalm and I find it interesting how often it focuses on time. Remember, Moses was the guy who led the children of Israel for forty years of wandering in the dessert because of their sin. I'm not sure if this was written before or after that, but Moses' life has something to teach us about time.

The Psalm begins by stating that the Lord is our dwelling place. He is our home base, security, and the one we run to in times of need. He has always been and always will be, never having been created. Then it says, "A thousand years in your sight are like a day that has just gone by, or like a watch in the night" (v. 4). Wow! No wonder we sometimes get impatient with God's timing. If 1,000 years are like a day to him, then he certainly has a bigger perspective than we do. Rather than being impatient, this helps us remember that he is working, even when we cannot see what he is doing.

Moses goes on to say, "Our days may come to seventy years, or eighty, if our strength endures" (v. 10). Our lives are but a moment in comparison to eternity. Then he says, "Teach us to number our days, that we may gain a heart of wisdom" (v. 12). There is something powerful about making our time on this earth count for eternity. It's interesting that the very common phrase "using your time wisely" brings up the very character quality that the psalmist mentions here-wisdom. A wise person is intentional with how they spend their days-especially their free time.

As our kids get older, I am more aware of how I spend my free time because it seems I have less of it. However, I find that time spent with the Lord, family, and friends fills me up more than anything else.

I think it's appropriate to end with verse fourteen which says, "Satisfy us in the morning with your unfailing love, that we may sing for joy and be glad all our days". When God's love satisfies us, we will be singing for joy the rest of our days.

Reflection Questions

1. How do you manage your time? Are you prone to being too planned or not planning enough?
2. How can you be wiser with your time management?

Lord, time is a gift from you that I want to use wisely to further your kingdom. Teach me to number my days in such a way that honors you and is a blessing to those around me.

DAY 2   Disc 2 / Track 7

Our Glorious God

The LORD reigns, let the earth be glad; let the distant shores rejoice. Clouds and thick darkness surround him; righteousness and justice are the foundation of his throne. Fire goes before him and consumes his foes on every side. His lightning lights up the world; the earth sees and trembles. The mountains melt like wax before the LORD, before the Lord of all the earth. The heavens proclaim his righteousness, and all peoples see his glory. All who worship images are put to shame, those who boast in idols—worship him, all you gods! Zion hears and rejoices and the villages of Judah are glad because of your judgments, LORD. For you, LORD, are the Most High over all the earth; you are exalted far above all gods. Let those who love the LORD hate evil, for he guards the lives of his faithful ones and delivers them from the hand of the wicked. Light shines on the righteous and joy on the upright in heart. Rejoice in the LORD, you who are righteous, and praise his holy name.

PSALM 97:1-12

This Psalm is all about the greatness and glory of the Lord. It says he reigns on high over the earth. Righteousness and justice are the pillars of his rule. He destroys his enemies.

"The heavens proclaim his righteousness, and all peoples see his glory" (v. 6). God's glory is made known for everyone to see. The question is, "Are we looking for it?"

Have you ever considered that we were created to reflect God's glory? In the book *Goliath Must Fall*, Giglio says, "We are designed to be dependent on our Creator and reflective of his greatness and glory." He goes on to say, "That's why glory is woven through every fiber of our being."[21]

That's why we love and are inspired by amazing athletes, musicians, movies, books, etc. We are drawn to glorious things that move us. They should point us to the one who made them. These other things pale in comparison to the greatness, glory, and power of the Lord!

Verses ten and eleven say, "Let those who love the Lord hate evil, for he guards the lives of his faithful ones and delivers them from the hand of the wicked. Light shines on the righteous and joy on the upright in heart." The Lord watches over us when we follow him. His light shines on us and we are filled with his joy!

Reflection Questions

1. What glorious things on this earth do you enjoy?
2. How can those things point you to the greater glory of the Lord?

Lord, you are glorious and your creation reflects your glory. When I am moved by amazing things on this earth, let them point me to your greater glory and power.

DAY 3 ⚹ 🔘 Disc 2 / Track 8

Sing to the Lord

I Sing to the LORD a new song, for he has done marvelous things; his right hand and his holy arm have worked salvation for him. The LORD has made his salvation known and revealed his righteousness to the nations. He has remembered his love and his faithfulness to Israel; all the ends of the earth have seen the salvation of our God. Shout for joy to the LORD, all the earth, burst into jubilant song with music; make music to the LORD with the harp, with the harp and the sound of singing, with trumpets and the blast of the ram's horn-shout for joy before the LORD, the King. Let the sea resound, and everything in it, the world, and all who live in it. Let the rivers clap their hands, let the mountains sing together for joy; let them sing before the LORD, for he comes to judge the earth. He will judge the world in righteousness and the peoples with equity.

PSALM 98:1-9

I have always loved to sing. My father loves to sing, and so did his father, my grandfather. You could say it was passed down to me. I grew up singing in choirs from elementary school through college, and I now get the privilege of leading choirs and worship teams. Why is singing so powerful? There are many reasons; one being it puts to music the things we feel so passionate about.

Scripture often encourages us to sing a new song to the Lord. A new song expresses the things God has done-often in our own lives. I will never get tired of thanking the Lord for setting me free from anxiety and obsessive thoughts. It was one of the most pivotal turning points in my life. I was so distraught, burdened, and overwhelmed. The Lord used a Christian counselor, friends, and the ministry of Arrow Leadership[22] to bring me to a new place of peace in my life.

This Psalm speaks of singing a new song to the Lord because of the marvelous things he has done. It says, "The Lord has made his salvation known and revealed his righteousness to the nations. He has remembered his love and his faithfulness to Israel; all the ends of the earth have seen the salvation of our God" (v. 2-3). The Lord showed his love and faithfulness to the people of Israel throughout the Bible. He has now made his salvation known to us by Jesus going to the cross and dying so our sins could be forgiven.

Shouting is a way of expressing our excitement or urgency about something. We shout at sporting events, to get our kids' attention, or to celebrate something. Verse four says, "Shout for joy to the LORD, all the earth, burst into jubilant song with music". Just as shouting is a normal part of our lives, so should shouting for joy to the Lord be a normal part of our worship.

The Psalm goes on to talk about worshiping the Lord with musical instruments. I find it is easy to express my love and gratefulness to the Lord playing an instrument. My emotions are easily expressed, and it brings me joy. Joy is a natural by-product of worshiping the Lord with the gifts he gives us. This Psalm ends by focusing on creation singing before the Lord, the King. Let's join them in song!

Reflection Questions

1. Has the Lord done great things in your life? If so, think of an example.
2. Do you love to sing and shout to the Lord in worship?

Lord, I love to sing my praise to you! Thank you for the gift of music as a way to express our thanksgiving and praise to you for who you are and what you have done.

DAY 4 ● Disc 2 / Track 9

A Grateful Heart

Shout for joy to the LORD, all the earth. Worship the LORD with glad-ness; come before him with joyful songs. Know that the LORD is God. It is he who made us, and we are his; we are his people, the sheep of his pasture. Enter his gates with thanksgiving and his courts with praise; give thanks to him and praise his name. For the LORD is good and his love endures forever; his faithfulness continues through all generations.

PSALM 100:1-5

Have you ever noticed the difference that gratitude makes in your life? So many people today are searching for what they don't have, and are never satisfied, while others are thankful for what they have. Spiritually, when we value the Lord above all else, we realize that ultimately all we need is him.

This short Psalm of praise focuses on the importance of coming into the Lord's presence with thanksgiving because of his goodness, and because his love and faithfulness endure forever.

When we come into a worship setting with a heart of thanksgiving to the Lord, we are able to hear his voice and receive from him. However, when we are focused on the things we wish were different in life, then it is difficult to worship him. Notice-it is a matter of perspective. The grateful person may have any number of negative things occurring in their life that they wish were different, but it doesn't hinder their worship.

This Psalm begins with a call for the whole earth to shout joyfully to the Lord because of who he is. When we have a clear picture of who God is, it changes the way we view everything else. This Psalm reminds us that our great God made us and that "we are his people, the sheep of his pasture" (v. 3). Since we are his creation, we should follow his plans and purposes for our lives. Our Shepherd watches over us, protects us, and leads us. We can be thankful to him at all times, knowing that he is with us.

Reflection Questions

1. What are you thankful for today?
2. How can gratitude change your perspective on your problems?

Father, thank you for loving me even though I don't deserve it. Thank you for my family and the friends you have put in my life. Thank you for your faithfulness to me at all times.

DAY 5   Disc 2 / Track 10

The Compassionate God

Hear my prayer, LORD; let my cry for help come to you. Do not hide your face from me when I am in distress. Turn your ear to me; when I call, answer me quickly. For my days vanish like smoke; my bones burn like glowing embers. My heart is blighted and withered like grass; I forget to eat my food. In my distress I groan aloud and am reduced to skin and bones. I am like a desert owl, like an owl among the ruins. I lie awake; I have become like a bird alone on a roof. All day long my enemies taunt me; those who rail against me use my name as a curse. For I eat ashes as my food and mingle my drink with tears because of your great wrath, for you have taken me up and thrown me aside. My days are like the evening shadow; I wither away like grass. But you, LORD, sit enthroned forever; your renown endures through all generations. You will arise and have compassion on Zion, for it is time to show favor to her; the appointed time has come. For her stones are dear to your servants; her very dust moves them to pity. The nations will fear the name of the Lord, all the kings of the earth will revere your glory. For the LORD will rebuild Zion and appear in his glory. He will respond to the prayer of the destitute; he will not despise their plea. Let this be written for a future generation, that a people not yet created may praise the LORD: "The Lord looked down from his sanctuary on high, from heaven he viewed the earth, to hear the groans of the prisoners and release those condemned to death." So the name of the LORD will be declared in Zion and his praise in Jerusalem when the peoples and the kingdoms assemble to worship the LORD

PSALM 102:1-22

The normal tendency for most people going through a difficult time is to turn inward, focus on their problems, and try to find a way out of them. This Psalm shows us how we should respond in those moments.

The psalmist is in a very tough spot and pours out his heart to the Lord. He says, "Do not hide your face from me when I am in distress. Turn your ear to me; when I call, answer me quickly" (v. 2). Sometimes it feels like God is hiding his face from us. Over and over again, scripture speaks of the light of God's face shining on someone as a blessing. No wonder it feels so horrible when we think God is hiding his face from us. The psalmist says that he forgets to eat, is groaning, and his enemies are making fun of him. He feels like God is responsible for what is happening to him.

However, then he shifts his focus from himself to the Lord. Verse twelve says, "But you, LORD sit enthroned forever; your renown endures through all generations" (v. 12). He begins to focus on the greatness and the compassion of the Lord. It says, "He will respond to the prayer of the destitute; he will not despise their plea" (v. 17). He knows that the Lord has compassion on him in his situation. As it says in Psalm 34:18, "The LORD is close to the brokenhearted and saves those who are crushed in spirit."

Rather than keeping his focus on his difficulties, the psalmist focuses on the Lord and his character. When we are tempted to feel sorry for ourselves and focus on our problems, we need to lift our eyes up to our great and compassionate God. Then it says that future generations will worship the Lord because of the deliverance he provided to the people of Israel. Isn't that how it works? When we tell of God's amazing work in our lives, it can be an encouragement to our children and the generations to come, about our great and compassionate God.

Reflection Questions

1. What do you do when problems surround you?
2. How can focusing on the Lord change your perspective on your troubles?

Father, thank you for being the great and compassionate God who is close to me in my time of need. When I am tempted to focus on my problems, help me to allow your greatness and glory to change my perspective.

DAY 6 ⬤ Disc 2 / Track 11

The Works of the Lord

Praise the LORD. I will extol the LORD with all my heart in the council of the upright and in the assembly. Great are the works of the LORD; they are pondered by all who delight in them. Glorious and majestic are his deeds, and his righteousness endures forever. He has caused his wonders to be remembered; the LORD is gracious and compassionate. He provides food for those who fear him; he remembers his covenant forever. He has shown his people the power of his works, giving them the lands of other nations. The works of his hands are faithful and just; all his precepts are trustworthy. They are established for ever and ever, enacted in faithfulness and uprightness. He provided redemption for his people; he ordained his covenant forever—holy and awesome is his name. The fear of the LORD is the beginning of wisdom; all who follow his precepts have good understanding. To him belongs eternal praise.

PSALM 111:1-10

Have you ever had the privilege of introducing someone who had an amazing resume'? Maybe their list of accomplishments and accolades was impressive. This Psalm is a list of the works of the Lord. It puts any human's accomplishments to shame.

The psalmist says, "Great are the works of the Lord; they are pondered by all who delight in them" (v. 2). When we take the time to think about the amazing things the Lord has done, we are filled with joy because of them. It helps us delight in the Lord!

What are these glorious and majestic works? He created the heavens and the earth by speaking them into existence. The Lord was faithful to the people of Israel throughout history and is faithful to us today. He is also full of grace and compassion. Verse five says, "He provides food for those who fear him". Those who follow the Lord will have their needs provided. "And my God will meet all your needs according to the riches of his glory in Christ Jesus" (Phil. 4:19).

Verse six says, the Lord showed his power to the nation of Israel by giving them the lands of the nations around them. The Lord gave them victory in their battles. It says that his works are faithful and just, and that he is trustworthy.

Sometimes we can wonder if God has forgotten about us or if our current challenges will turn out for good. However, we can take hope, knowing that the God who was faithful to his people throughout history, will be faithful to us today.

This Psalm ends by saying, "The fear of the LORD is the beginning of wisdom; all who follow his precepts have good understanding. To him belongs eternal praise" (v. 10). If we want to be wise then we will honor, love, and respect the Lord first in our lives even when we don't understand what he is doing.

It is fitting that this Psalm ends in verse ten by mentioning "eternal praise" to God for his amazing works. We would be wise to exalt the Lord daily for the awesome deeds he has done and is doing all around us!

Reflection Questions

1. Do you spend time thinking about God's amazing works? If not, what can help you do that?

2. How can reflecting on God's works give you hope in your current struggles?

Lord, I am impressed with all you have done throughout history and with what you are doing today. I'm thankful that you are faithful to your people. I exalt you today for your amazing works!

DAY 7 Disc 2 / Track 12

From the Rising to the Setting

Praise the LORD. Praise the LORD, you his servants; praise the name of the LORD. Let the name of the LORD be praised, both now and forevermore. From the rising of the sun to the place where it sets, the name of the LORD is to be praised. The LORD is exalted over all the nations, his glory above the heavens. Who is like the LORD our God, the One who sits enthroned on high, who stoops down to look on the heavens and the earth? He raises the poor from the dust and lifts the needy from the ash heap; he seats them with princes, with the princes of his people. He settles the childless woman in her home as a happy mother of children. Praise the LORD.

PSALM 113:1-9

Have you ever seen a sunrise or sunset that was absolutely breathtaking? It is an amazing, colorful sight to see. The Lord made those for us to enjoy and to get a small glimpse of his glory.

This Psalm proclaims the Lord is worthy of praise from where the sun rises, to the place it sets in the evening. In other words, the Lord is to be worshiped at all times! The question is, "Are we taking time throughout our days to acknowledge his greatness?".

Then the psalmist proclaims that the Lord is above all peoples and the creation he has made by saying, "The LORD is exalted over all the nations, his glory above the heavens" (v. 4). There is no created being or work that surpasses his greatness. There is no one like him. He is the true king, exalted above all.

However, in all his greatness and glory he stoops down to look at us. He considers us, loves us, and cares for us. He is the compassionate God who looks after the poor and lifts them up. It says that the Lord shows his love to the childless woman by giving her the blessing of children.

I am always amazed at the way Jesus treated people when he was on the earth. He considered it his mission to meet their spiritual and physical needs. His primary concern was their spiritual needs, but he went out of his way to heal the sick, cast out demons, and to give people hope as they put their faith in him.

We have also been given the mission to preach the gospel and to meet the spiritual and the physical needs of people. Recently, a hurricane has been ravaging Texas and other states as well. Right now, nothing speaks louder to the victims than providing food, shelter, and help during their time of need. At this time, those things speak loudest to them about the love of Jesus.

Even as we love and serve other people we must remember that ultimately, we are doing it as worship to the Lord! "So whether you eat or drink or whatever you do, do it all for the glory of God" (I Cor. 10:31).

Reflection Questions

1. Do you take time to worship the Lord during the day? If not, what can help you do that?
2. How does God's compassion and love for the needy call you to action?

Father, you are exalted above all, worthy of praise at all times, and there is no one like you. I am amazed that you take time to show your love to those in need. I choose to follow your example by taking time to love the poor and needy around me.

WEEK

6

Glory to Your Name

Not to us, LORD, not to us but to your name be the glory, because of your love and faithfulness. Why do the nations say, "Where is their God?" Our God is in heaven; he does whatever pleases him. But their idols are silver and gold, made by human hands. They have mouths, but cannot speak, eyes, but cannot see. They have ears, but cannot hear, noses, but cannot smell. They have hands, but cannot feel, feet, but cannot walk, nor can they utter a sound with their throats. Those who make them will be like them, and so will all who trust in them. All you Israelites, trust in the LORD—he is their help and shield. House of Aaron, trust in the LORD— he is their help and shield. You who fear him, trust in the LORD—he is their help and shield. The LORD remembers us and will bless us: He will bless his people Israel, he will bless the house of Aaron, he will bless those who fear the LORD—small and great alike. May the LORD cause you to flourish, both you and your children. May you be blessed by the LORD, the Maker of heaven and earth. The highest heavens belong to the LORD, but the earth he has given to mankind. It is not the dead who praise the LORD, those who go down to the place of silence; it is we who extol the LORD, both now and forevermore. Praise the LORD.

PSALM 115:1-18

Many people today live for the praises and accolades of others. We are all tempted to value the approval of others too highly. This Psalm puts this in perspective saying, "Not to us, LORD, not to us but to your name be the glory, because of your love and faithfulness" (v. 1). To the people of Israel, this was a reminder about everything the Lord had done for them.[23] When we consider the Lord's love and faithfulness, and our weaknesses in those areas, we realize he deserves all the praise. That is just one example that puts our relationship to him in perspective.

The psalmist compares the one true God of Israel to the false idols of the surrounding nations. Our God is in heaven and does as he pleases. However, their gods cannot talk, see, hear, smell, feel, walk, etc. They were made by humans and it says, "Those who make them will be like them, and so will all who trust in them" (v. 8). Basically, those who make them and trust in them will be as powerless as they are.

Then there is a charge for Israel and for us today to trust in God our helper and protector, the one who will bless us. There are times when I am tempted to put my trust in other things when I feel like the Lord isn't going to come through in an area. Some examples of this are putting my trust in finances, opportunities, or relationships. However, this Psalm reminds all of us that God longs to bless us, but we ultimately need to trust him as our source, even when he doesn't provide in the ways we want him to.

The psalmist ends where he started by giving glory to the Lord. He says, "It is we who extol the Lord, both now and forevermore. Praise the LORD" (v. 18).

Reflection Questions

1. In what ways has the Lord blessed you?
2. How does the Lord get more glory when we trust him with our lives?

Lord you deserve all the praise, honor, and glory! Thank you for the faithfulness and love you have shown me. I am thankful that I can trust you with everything in my life. I choose to trust you today with _____.

DAY 2

The God who Delivers

Give thanks to the LORD, for he is good; his love endures forever. Let Israel say: "His love endures forever." Let the house of Aaron say: "His love endures forever." Let those who fear the LORD say: "His love endures forever." When hard pressed, I cried to the LORD; he brought me into a spacious place. The LORD is with me; I will not be afraid. What can mere mortals do to me? The LORD is with me; he is my helper. I look in triumph on my enemies. It is better to take refuge in the LORD than to trust in humans. It is better to take refuge in the LORD than to trust in princes. All the nations surrounded me, but in the name of the LORD I cut them down. They surrounded me on every side, but in the name of the LORD I cut them down. They swarmed around me like bees, but they were consumed as quickly as burning thorns; in the name of the LORD I cut them down. I was pushed back and about to fall, but the LORD helped me. The LORD is my strength and my defense; he has become my salvation. Shouts of joy and victory resound in the tents of the righteous: "The LORD's right hand has done mighty things! The LORD's right hand is lifted high; the LORD's right hand has done mighty things!" I will not die but live, and will proclaim what the LORD has done. The LORD has chastened me severely, but he has not given me over to death. Open for me the gates of the righteous; I will enter and give thanks to the LORD. This is the gate of the LORD through which the righteous may enter. I will give you thanks, for you answered me; you have become my salvation.

PSALM 118:1-21

Have you ever felt trapped or suffocated by something or someone? Sometimes we feel that no matter what choice we make-trouble awaits us. For instance, no matter how well we treat people, they won't always like or approve of the decisions we make and that can cause trouble in the relationship. This can cause great fear in our lives if we allow it to.

This Psalm of thanksgiving focuses on the Lord's goodness and love to Israel and to all who fear him. It says, "When hard pressed, I cried to the Lord; he brought me into a spacious place" (v. 5). When under attack we can feel stuck or trapped, but the Lord brings us "into a spacious place". I love that word picture. I think of a wide, open field or somewhere where we are free from danger, confinement, and trouble. The Lord delivers us from evil and gives us peace.

Then it says that because the Lord is with us we don't have to be afraid of people. Just let that thought sink in for a moment. I would guess most of us allow the fear of others to affect us more than we realize. This Psalm reminds us that people are powerless before God.

I think of Shadrach, Meshach, and Abednego when they told King Nebuchadnezzar that they wouldn't bow down and worship his golden idol, knowing they would be killed. They said, "If we are thrown into the blazing furnace, the God we serve is able to deliver us from it, and he will deliver us from Your Majesty's hand. But even if he does not, we want you to know, Your Majesty, that we will not serve your gods or worship the image of gold you have set up" (Dan. 3:17-18).

How did they have the courage to respond that way? They knew that ultimately the king was powerless before God, and the Lord did deliver them from the fiery furnace.

The psalmist tells us that because the Lord is with us we will be victorious. It is always better to take refuge in and trust in the Lord then to put our hope in people. They will sometimes let us down, but the Lord will not.

The Lord helped his people in their battles against their enemies and then they took time to proclaim what he had done. "Shouts of joy and victory resound in the tents of the righteous: 'The Lord's right hand has done mighty things!' I will not die but live, and will proclaim what the Lord has done" (vv. 15,17).

How often do we forget or neglect to tell others about the amazing things the Lord has done? There are many times when we literally would've died if it weren't for the protecting hand of the Lord and his angels in our lives. Let's declare with thanksgiving what he has done. It gives him glory and builds the faith of those around us!

Reflection Questions

1. Have you ever felt trapped by something or someone? What did you do?
2. How can you have the strength to trust God like Shadrach, Meshach, and Abednego?

Father, you are the all-powerful God who is my help and salvation. I choose not to fear people or situations around me, instead choosing to trust you with my life and all I have.

DAY 3   Disc 2 / Track 15

The House of the Lord

I rejoiced with those who said to me, "Let us go to the house of the LORD."
Our feet are standing in your gates, Jerusalem. Jerusalem is built like a
city that is closely compacted together. That is where the tribes go up—
the tribes of the LORD—to praise the name of the LORD according to
the statute given to Israel. There stand the thrones for judgment, the
thrones of the house of David. Pray for the peace of Jerusalem: "May
those who love you be secure. May there be peace within your walls and
security within your citadels." For the sake of my family and friends, I
will say, "Peace be within you." For the sake of the house of the LORD our
God, I will seek your prosperity.

PSALM 122:1-9

This Psalm focuses on Jerusalem as it was the Israelites' place of
worship. They would travel to Jerusalem to worship. Verse one says,
"I rejoiced with those who said to me, 'Let us go to the house of the
Lord'". They were excited to worship the Lord in his dwelling place.
Do we eagerly anticipate gathering with the church and worshiping
the Lord with his people?

Thankfully, we can praise the Lord from any location, but there
is something special about worshiping him with his people. There is
also great power in the church coming together to worship the Lord.
Psalm 133:1 says, "How good and pleasant it is when God's people
live together in unity". This includes when we worship together in
unity. God often answers prayer, performs miracles, and delivers his
people when they are coming together and exalting him.

The second half of the Psalm directs our attention to the peace
of Jerusalem. "Pray for the peace of Jerusalem: 'May those who love

you be secure. May there be peace within your walls and security within your citadels'" (vv. 6-7). They valued peace in their central city of worship. We should pray for the peace and unity in the church today so that we can be effective in our mission of telling people about the love of Jesus.

In Matthew 12:25 Jesus says that a divided kingdom or house won't stand. The same is true of the church. When we are gossiping, backbiting, and fighting each other, we lose our effectiveness. In those instances, the world doesn't like what it sees. However, when the church comes together in unity to love Jesus and proclaim the gospel, the world takes notice. They may not agree with our message, but they take notice when we love each other!

Reflection Questions

1. Do you eagerly anticipate gathering with the church to worship? Why or why not?
2. Why is it important to pray for the peace and unity of the church?

Lord, I love your church and am thankful to be a part of it. I pray for the peace and unity of the church, so we can be effective at telling others about your saving grace.

DAY 4 ※ ● Disc 2 / Track 16

Our Escape

If the LORD had not been on our side—let Israel say—if the LORD had not been on our side when people attacked us, they would have swallowed us alive when their anger flared against us; the flood would have engulfed us, the torrent would have swept over us, the raging waters would have swept us away. Praise be to the LORD, who has not let us be torn by their teeth. We have escaped like a bird from the fowler's snare; the snare has been broken, and we have escaped. Our help is in the name of the LORD, the Maker of heaven and earth.

PSALM 124:1-8

How many times have you said, "If God hadn't helped in this situation, then _____ would've happened"? I have said that many times. My wife was in a car accident last year when an out of control car was coming directly for her stopped vehicle. She was able to quickly move the car about ten feet so that the impact came behind her driver's door. I know the Lord was protecting her in that moment and it wasn't by chance that she had open space to move the car into. The car had to be totaled, and other than being sore, she was ok.

This Psalm presents many scenarios like my story. If God wasn't on their side when Israel was attacked, they would've been swallowed alive and the flood waters would've swept over them.

It also says, "Praise be to the Lord, who has not let us be torn by their teeth. We have escaped like a bird from the fowler's snare; the snare has been broken, and we have escaped" (vv. 6-7). This analogy makes me think of the dog our family had when I was growing up. Teddy was an Airedale who was hyper, friendly, and he loved to hunt. On one occasion, he killed a raccoon. Another time he caught a squirrel falling from a tree, and it was alive in his mouth. The last thing he wanted to do was give up his prize. It was nearly impossible to pry open his mouth when he had his prey in it.

This helps me understand the impact of what the psalmist is saying when he talks about escaping from the teeth of the enemy. The Lord helped them escape like a bird caught in the mouth of the enemy. In a much greater way than an animal escaping from the jaws of my dog (which was something), the Lord helped Israel escape from the trap set by their enemy. The Lord is truly our help in times of need!

Reflection Questions

1. Do you have any "if _____, then _____" God stories? Think of one.
2. How can stories like this increase your trust in the Lord?

Father, thank you for the many times your hand of protection has saved me and those I love from disaster. I am so glad you do not leave me alone, but you help me in my time of need.

Like a Child

My heart is not proud, LORD, my eyes are not haughty; I do not concern myself with great matters or things too wonderful for me. But I have calmed and quieted myself, I am like a weaned child with its mother; like a weaned child I am content. Israel, put your hope in the LORD both now and forevermore.

PSALM 131:1-3

There are many things that we cannot fully understand here on this earth. There are some mysteries that we will need to ask the Lord about when we get to Heaven. If we spend too much of our time and energy trying to figure out things we cannot fully understand in this life, we may be concerning ourselves with things too wonderful for us. Here the psalmist mentions that the proud person elevates themselves by concerning themselves with things that are in the Lord's hands. If we try to be the master of our own destiny or in any way usurp God's authority in our lives, we will be filled with pride.

On the other hand, the humble person is filled with peace as they trust in the Lord, knowing their life is in his hands. Verse two says, "But I have calmed and quieted myself, I am like a weaned child with its mother; like a weaned child I am content." A child who is no longer nursing is content with solid foods and with the security of their relationship to their mother. In the same way, when we are content in our relationship with the Lord, our desire for the sinful things of this world diminishes.

The apostle Paul talks about contentment by saying, "I know what it is to be in need, and I know what it is to have plenty. I have learned the secret of being content in any and every situation" (Phil. 4:12). Paul understood that contentment wasn't based on the things around him, but it was based on whom he was trusting.

Recently, my friend passed away from a sudden massive heart attack. We have all been mourning his loss. His wife mentioned to me that he kept things simple in life and didn't complicate them. He knew what he liked and didn't like, but most of all, his life exemplified a trust in the Lord. This Psalm makes me think of him, because it describes someone who is at peace.

Sometimes I complicate things by examining every option, possibility, and meaning. At the end of the day, in whom am I trusting? The Psalm ends by encouraging us to put our "hope in the Lord" (v. 3) forever.

Reflection Questions

1. How can pride creep into our lives?
2. How much peace are you experiencing in your life these days?

Father, help me to have faith like a child when it comes to trusting you. Rather than complicating things, I simply choose to trust.

DAY 6   Disc 2 / Track 18

Sovereign Lord

Rescue me, LORD, from evildoers; protect me from the violent, who devise evil plans in their hearts and stir up war every day. They make their tongues as sharp as a serpent's; the poison of vipers is on their lips. Keep me safe, LORD, from the hands of the wicked; protect me from the violent, who devise ways to trip my feet. The arrogant have hidden a snare for me; they have spread out the cords of their net and have set traps for me along my path. I say to the LORD, "You are my God." Hear, LORD, my cry for mercy. Sovereign LORD, my strong deliverer, you shield my head in the day of battle. Do not grant the wicked their desires, LORD; do not let their plans succeed. Those who surround me proudly rear their heads; may the mischief of their lips engulf them. May burning coals fall on them; may they be thrown into the fire, into miry pits, never to rise. May slanderers not be established in the land; may disaster hunt down the violent. I know that the LORD secures justice for the poor and upholds the cause of the needy. Surely the righteous will praise your name, and the upright will live in your presence.

PSALM 140:1-13

Have you ever been around someone who stirs up problems wherever they go? Some of our personalities are actually wired to solve problems however, we can create problems if we are not careful.

In this Psalm David is asking God to save him from evil people who want to cause him harm. They are stirring up problems with the things they say and do. They are trying to trap him. We can relate to David when we feel like people are trying to cause us harm. What should we do in those situations?

David says, "I say to the Lord, 'You are my God.' Hear, Lord, my cry for mercy. Sovereign Lord, my strong deliverer, you shield my head in the day of battle. Do not grant the wicked their desires, Lord; do not let their plans succeed" (vv. 6-8). David shifts his focus to the one who holds the power-the Lord. He calls on the Sovereign (all-powerful) Lord for help. Just like a helmet protected a warrior in battle, the Lord protected David from things that could destroy him.

We need to place our focus on the Lord when people are coming against us. Ultimately people aren't our enemy as Paul reminds us. "For we do not wrestle against flesh and blood, but against the rulers, against the authorities, against the cosmic powers over this present darkness, against the spiritual forces of evil in the heavenly places" (Eph. 6:12-ESV).

David ends this Psalm by contrasting the wicked with two qualities that those who love and serve the Lord possess. They praise his name and live in his presence. If God is truly our focus in life, difficulties with people will cause us to worship him and seek his presence in greater ways. Our challenges with people can actually cause us to experience greater joy and intimacy with the Lord if we allow him to change us in the process.

Reflection Questions

1. How do you react when people are attacking you?
2. How can shifting your focus to the Lord help you gain perspective when dealing with people?

Lord, I realize that ultimately, people are not my enemy. I choose to run to you when I feel that I am being mistreated or attacked. Build my character as I allow you to change me.

DAY 7 ● Disc 2 / Track 19

Hear My Complaint

With my voice I cry out to the LORD; with my voice I plead for mercy to the LORD. I pour out my complaint before him; I tell my trouble before him. When my spirit faints within me, you know my way! In the path where I walk they have hidden a trap for me. Look to the right and see: there is none who takes notice of me; no refuge remains to me; no one cares for my soul. I cry to you, O LORD; I say, "You are my refuge, my portion in the land of the living." Attend to my cry, for I am brought very low! Deliver me from my persecutors, for they are too strong for me! Bring me out of prison, that I may give thanks to your name! The righteous will surround me, for you will deal bountifully with me.

PSALM 142:1-7 (ESV)

Do you ever feel completely frustrated with life's demands or troubles? When I sat down to write this devotional I was feeling overwhelmed and frustrated about many things. I found it interesting that that was what the psalmist was feeling in this chapter. He is crying out to God for mercy and says, "I pour out my complaint before him; I tell my trouble before him" (v. 2-ESV). Are we completely honest with God about our troubles? He already knows about them before we tell him, but it helps us to express it to him in prayer.

The psalmist goes on to say that when we feel exhausted and overwhelmed, the Lord knows our heart. He knows when we are innocent before our enemies.[24] Verse four (ESV) says, "Look to the right and see: there is none who takes notice of me; no refuge remains to me; no one cares for my soul." The psalmist is alone and desolate as he calls to the Lord for help.

There are scriptures where the Lord is described as being at our right hand as our protector like Psalm 110:5: "The Lord is at your right hand; he will crush kings on the day of his wrath." Even though people weren't there to protect him, the almighty, powerful Lord was.

He describes his situation as if he is in prison asking to be released. Sometimes we feel imprisoned by our worries and challenges, but things change when we truly give them over to the Lord. When I yield my worries and the outcome of them to the Lord, I don't have to carry the weight of them anymore. Just this week I was worried about the loss of a volunteer team member and was desperately trying to find a replacement. I was in a worried frenzy; however, then I realized that God had already provided a temporary solution to the problem. I stopped worrying, remembering that God is in control and that he is the provider.

There is a difference between being hardworking and responsible and being in a frantic frenzy to fix things. Our frantic episodes don't usually signify trust in the Lord. Let's remember that as the Lord helped the psalmist, he will help us in our difficulties as well.

Reflection Questions

1. Are you completely honest with God about your complaints and your troubles? Why or why not?
2. In your frantic moments, what can help you give your worries to the Lord?

Lord today my complaint is about _____. I yield the entire situation to you. Give me your perspective on it and your course of action. Thank you for hearing my prayer.

BONUS

DAY 1   Disc 2 / Track 20

Remember His Works

LORD, hear my prayer, listen to my cry for mercy; in your faithfulness and righteousness come to my relief. Do not bring your servant into judgment, for no one living is righteous before you. The enemy pursues me, he crushes me to the ground; he makes me dwell in the darkness like those long dead. So my spirit grows faint within me; my heart within me is dismayed. I remember the days of long ago; I meditate on all your works and consider what your hands have done. I spread out my hands to you; I thirst for you like a parched land. Answer me quickly, LORD; my spirit fails. Do not hide your face from me or I will be like those who go down to the pit. Let the morning bring me word of your unfailing love, for I have put my trust in you. Show me the way I should go, for to you I entrust my life. Rescue me from my enemies, LORD, for I hide myself in you. Teach me to do your will, for you are my God; may your good Spirit lead me on level ground. For your name's sake, LORD, preserve my life; in your righteousness, bring me out of trouble. In your unfailing love, silence my enemies; destroy all my foes, for I am your servant.

PSALM 143:1-12

Do you ever get so focused on your present circumstances and activities that you find it hard to remember the past or look to the future? Sometimes this happens simply because of busyness, but other times I get so hyperfocused on my current challenges, that I struggle to think about anything else.

In this Psalm David is asking the Lord to hear him and to respond because of his faithfulness and righteousness. Then he immediately asks for mercy. David knew that his best efforts were far from God's holy standard.

He begins to talk about his enemies and the trouble they are causing him. He says, "The enemy pursues me, he crushes me to the ground; he makes me dwell in the darkness like those long dead. So my spirit grows faint within me; my heart within me is dismayed" (vv. 3-4). Do you ever feel completely discouraged because of something going on in your life? In those moments, we can get so focused on our discouragement that we miss all the wonderful things going on around us.

Here David says, "I remember the days of long ago; I meditate on all your works and consider what your hands have done. I spread out my hands to you; I thirst for you like a parched land" (vv. 5-6). He looked back and remembered all the Lord had done for him. He thought about and pondered what God had done and then he began to seek the Lord. What an amazing change takes place! One minute he is completely focused on his problems, but as he remembers the Lord's provision and faithfulness to him in the past, he begins to seek after God like one hungers and thirsts for food and drink.

When I am focused on my difficulties, in my discouragement, I find it hard to seek after the Lord. However, when I remember his faithfulness to me in the past, it stirs up a hunger in my heart for more of him in the present.

David goes on to affirm his trust in the Lord and then he says, "For your name's sake, Lord, preserve my life" (v. 11). What a great reminder that everything is for his glory and honor. All of our struggles and difficulties are ultimately meant to give God glory in one way or another.

Reflection Questions

1. *Do you ever get hyperfocused on your challenges? If so, what causes discouragement in those moments?*
2. *How can remembering the Lord's work in the past encourage you today?*

Lord I confess that sometimes my faith is weak and I struggle to trust you. When I get overwhelmed with difficulties, help me remember who you are and everything you have done in the past. Lord, build my faith.

DAY 2 ● Disc 2 / Track 21

Glory Beyond Comparison

Praise the LORD. Praise the LORD from the heavens; praise him in the heights above. Praise him, all his angels; praise him, all his heavenly hosts. Praise him, sun and moon; praise him, all you shining stars. Praise him, you highest heavens and you waters above the skies. Let them praise the name of the LORD, for at his command they were created, and he established them for ever and ever—he issued a decree that will never pass away. Praise the LORD from the earth, you great sea creatures and all ocean depths, lightning and hail, snow and clouds, stormy winds that do his bidding, you mountains and all hills, fruit trees and all cedars, wild animals and all cattle, small creatures and flying birds, kings of the earth and all nations, you princes and all rulers on earth, young men and women, old men and children. Let them praise the name of the LORD, for his name alone is exalted; his splendor is above the earth and the heavens. And he has raised up for his people a horn, the praise of all his faithful servants, of Israel, the people close to his heart. Praise the LORD.

PSALM 148:1-14

After reading this Psalm I took a step back to think about its practical implications in my life. Do I really understand the greatness of the Lord? What is this Psalm of praise calling us to today?

I tend to compartmentalize greatness in my thinking. There are local athletes, musicians, business leaders, and other movers and shakers who have achieved a level of success in their field. The same is true on the regional, state, national, and international levels. We can be impressed with amazing talent at any level. However, this Psalm reminds us that the Lord's greatness and power is so far above his creation that we cannot comprehend it. Sometimes we're too easily impressed with manmade things that will fade away. However, the best of our work and achievements should be pointers to the greatness and glory of our Creator.

This Psalm of praise begins by calling the Lord's creation "in the heights above" (v. 1) to worship him. This includes the heavens, angels, heavenly hosts, sun, moon, stars, etc. Then it focuses on the earth below. The sea creatures, ocean depths, the weather, every animal, and all peoples great and small are called to praise his name. Like Psalm 8:2 reminds us, we truly were created to worship the Lord from the womb.

Verse thirteen says, "Let them praise the name of the Lord, for his name alone is exalted; his splendor is above the earth and the heavens." Only the name of the Lord is worthy of praise. It's interesting that when Moses asked to see God's glory the Lord said, "'I will cause all my goodness to pass in front of you, and I will proclaim my name, the Lord, in your presence'" (Ex. 33:19).

His name is representative of his glory and his greatness. That's one reason we have so many names in scripture describing the many facets of the Lord's character. We use his different names to praise him for the many different qualities he has. Finally, his glory is so great that Moses could only see his back from a cleft of a rock. He would have died had he seen the Lord's face. This is a wonderful reminder of how great the glory of the Lord is.

Do we live our lives to showcase the glory of the Lord? In other words, do our actions, decisions, and way of life draw attention and point towards his greatness? Let's join with all of creation above and on the earth in exalting him today!

Reflection Questions

1. What does greatness mean to you? What impresses you?
2. Does your life showcase the glory of the Lord? How can you do that in greater ways?

Father, your glory and greatness are beyond my comprehension. Forgive me for being too impressed with things of this earth that will fade away. Give me a greater, more accurate view of your glory today.

DAY 3   Disc 2 / Track 22

Joy Unspeakable

Praise the LORD. Sing to the LORD a new song, his praise in the assembly of his faithful people. Let Israel rejoice in their Maker; let the people of Zion be glad in their King. Let them praise his name with dancing and make music to him with timbrel and harp. For the LORD takes delight in his people; he crowns the humble with victory. Let his faithful people rejoice in this honor and sing for joy on their beds. May the praise of God be in their mouths and a double-edged sword in their hands, to inflict vengeance on the nations and punishment on the peoples, to bind their kings with fetters, their nobles with shackles of iron, to carry out the sentence written against them—this is the glory of all his faithful people. Praise the LORD.

PSALM 149:1-9

We have been seeking to delight in the Lord in greater ways through this devotional. The question for many of us is how we can keep our focus on the truths of scripture when challenges emerge.

This Psalm of praise is full of joy as it speaks about rejoicing, gladness, and delight. It is a call to "sing a new song" (v. 1) to the Lord with his people and to rejoice in our King. Then it talks about praising the Lord with instruments and dancing. How can we have this kind of joy in our lives?

I recently read a short biography about William Wilberforce, the Christian politician in England, who fought against slavery and the slave trade for forty-seven years. He endured many difficult times and persecution from those who stood against him. However, he was an amazingly joyful person. That fact took me by surprise, because he endured so much difficulty.

Piper describes him in his book *Amazing Grace in the Life of Wil-*

liam Wilberforce by saying, "There was in this childlike love of children and joyful freedom from care a deeply healthy self-forgetfulness."[25] He loved to play with children and seemed to forget about his important position in society. Piper goes on to describe his delight in the Lord: "The durable delights in God and the desires for the fullness of Christ that sustained Wilberforce's life did not just happen."[26] Wilberforce spent much time in prayer and reading the Bible.

What a wonderful example of delighting in the Lord Wilberforce is for us today. He didn't allow the pressures of life to diminish his joy in God, and neither should we.

This Psalm reminds us that the Lord delights in us! "For the Lord takes delight in his people; he crowns the humble with victory" (v. 4). He takes delight in those who seek him and he blesses the path of the humble.

As I have journeyed through the Psalms again, seeking more guidance in learning to delight in the Lord, I have seen that there are many facets to this process. Each new situation in life brings with it a choice. We can choose to find our joy in the Lord, or look elsewhere for it. Just as the Lord led the psalmists and his people Israel, he will lead us too. As long as we are putting him first, joyfully seeking him, and giving him glory, we will remain on the path he has for us. I hope this devotional has encouraged you in this. Blessings on the journey ahead!

Reflection Questions

1. How can you become a more childlike, self-forgetful person?
2. Has your delight in the Lord increased while reading this devotional? If so, how can that continue?

Lord I am encouraged by others who have trusted you throughout history. Thank you for the gift of the Psalms as they teach me how to delight in you. I rejoice in your faithfulness, grace, and blessings in my life today. Give me a childlike heart as I desire to follow you with everything inside of me!

Endnotes

1. Kenneth L. Barker, *New International Version Study Bible*, (Grand Rapids, Mi.: Zondervan, 1985, 1995, 2002), 1055.

2. Ibid., 1056.

3. Exodus. 33-34.

4. Jonathan Edwards, *"The Christian Pilgrim,"* in The Works of Jonathan Edwards, ed. Edward Hickman, 2 vols. (1843; reprint, Edinburgh: Banner of Truth, 1974) 2:244.

5. Kenneth L. Barker, *New International Version Study Bible*, 1058.

6. Sinclair B. Ferguson, *The Power of Words and the Wonder of God*, Ed. John Piper and Justin Taylor (Wheaton, Ill.: Crossway, 2009), 54-55.

7. Hebrews 11:25.

8. Kenneth L. Barker, *New International Version Study Bible*, 1077.

9. Ibid., 1081.

10. Ibid., 1089.

11. Ibid., 1090.

12. John Piper Sermons–*We Need Each Other: Christian Fellowship as a Means of Perseverance*-April 18, 2017, 44 min, DesiringGod.com.

13. Jamieson-Fausset-Brown, *Psalms. Jamieson-Fausset-Brown Bible Commentary (Complete)*. N.p. (1871), http://www.biblestudytools.com/commentaries/jamieson-fausset-brown/psalms-1-75/.

14. Ibid., http://www.biblestudytools.com/commentaries/jamieson-fausset-brown/psalms-1-75/.

15. Kenneth L. Barker, *New International Version Study Bible*, 1131.

16. Jamieson-Fausset-Brown, *Psalms. Jamieson-Fausset-Brown Bible Commentary (Complete)*. N.p. (1871), http://www.biblestudytools.com/commentaries/jamieson-fausset-brown/psalms-1-75/.

17. My thoughts on this have been influenced by Tommy Walker's song "Make it Glorious" and his explanation of it. (Written by Tommy Walker, 2003 Integrity's Praise! Music, (Admin. By Capitol CMG Publishing (Integrity Music (DC Cook))) WeMobile Music (Admin. By Capitol CMG Publishing (Integrity Music (DC Cook)))

18. Kenneth L. Barker, *New International Version Study Bible*, 1150.

19. Ibid., 1180.

20. Fred W. Meuser, *Luther the Preacher* (Minneapolis: Augsburg Publishing House, 1983) 27.

21. Taken from *[Goliath Must Fall]* by [Louie Giglio] Copyright © [2017] by [Louie Giglio]. 231 Used by permission of Thomas Nelson. www.thomasnelson.com.

22. The Arrow Leadership program trains Christian leaders in North America and beyond to be "led more by Jesus, lead more like Jesus and lead more to Jesus." www.arrowleadership.org

23. Kenneth L. Barker, *New International Version Study Bible*, 1228.

24. Jamieson-Fausset-Brown, *Psalms. Jamieson-Fausset-Brown Bible Commentary (Complete)*. N.p. (1871), http://www.biblestudytools.com/commentaries/jamieson-fausset-brown/psalms-76-150/.

25. John Piper, *Amazing Grace in the Life of William Wilberforce* (Wheaton, Ill: Crossway Books, 2002) 64-digital copy.

26. Ibid., 71-digital copy.